FOR SUCH A TIME AS THIS

The liberation of women to lead in the church

Martin Scott

P.S. Promotions Ltd
Dover Park Drive
London SW15 5DG

FOR SUCH A TIME AS THIS

Copyright © Martin Scott November 2000

All Rights Reserved

Unless otherwise stated, all Scripture quotations are taken from
the HOLY BIBLE, NEW INTERNATIONAL VERSION.
Copyright © 1973, 1978, 1984 by the International Bible Society

ISBN 0 9539902 0 6

First Published February 2001 by
P.S. Promotions Ltd
3 Divis Way Dover Park Drive
London SW15 5DG

Printed in Great Britain by Unity Print Ltd

FOR SUCH A TIME AS THIS

The liberation of women to lead in the church

Contents

Preface		1
Chapter 1	By what authority?	7
Chapter 2	Leading in the church: which church?	23
Chapter 3	Women and woman in the Bible	35
Chapter 4	For the sake of the gospel	67
Chapter 5	Reading the Bible	89
Chapter 6	Restrictive passages	107
Chapter 7	Jesus: the male redeemer	151
Chapter 8	For such a time as this	165
Appendices		173
Appendix 1	Pentecostal women in ministry:-where do we go from here (Sheri R. Benvenuti)	175
Appendix 2		189
Bibliography		191

Preface

The subject of women in leadership within the church is a challenging one. Not only are theological and biblical issues raised, but emotional ones as well. To compound issues further it is not simply a challenging issue but is also a somewhat complex one for it forces us to address other aspects of our faith. In 1992 Word UK / Pioneer published *The Role and Ministry of Women* in which I sought to answer the key issue of the nature of authority before addressing the so-called 'difficult Scriptures' that we find in the Pauline material; this current publication is only in part a republication of that work as I will seek to address other related issues that I now believe are also critical.

In that previous publication I noted that 'much of the teaching on the role of women centres around the issue of authority', with questions as to the appropriateness of a woman exercising authority, and devoted the first chapter to that issue. I will do likewise in this publication but will then address the related issue of our distinctive church traditions and the specific question that each tradition must answer (chapter 2). Chapter 3 will give an outline of women and woman throughout Scripture. The creation narratives and Jesus' response to women will receive the greater attention here, although the results of the Fall, women in the Hebrew Scriptures and Paul's response to women will also feature. The presence of missiological principles within the New Testament in giving women a specific position will be addressed in chapter 4, which will naturally lead into an exploration of suitable hermeneutical principles[1] to apply in approaching Scripture on women, their status, position and role (chapter 5). I consider that the so-called 'difficult texts' should be looked at once the hermeneutical principles have been examined

---

[1] I ask the reader not to be put off by the use of certain technical words such as 'missiological' or 'hermeneutical'. The former describes principles that are applied in order to reach people with the gospel message; the latter describes the principles by which Scripture is interpreted. Such words will either be explained as the book unfolds or their meaning will become clear.

1

(chapter 6). Finally, prior to a summarising chapter the significance of the maleness of our Redeemer will be addressed.

It is perhaps in order at this stage to mention my approach to Scripture (although this will become apparent in the book, particularly in chapters 4-6). I believe that God has given us canonical Scripture which must be the rule that is applied to both our doctrine and practice. I do not believe that we can dismiss any text simply because we do not agree with it — we must come under the scrutiny of Scripture rather than the other way round. I will seek to exegete the pertinent texts, but I will also wish to understand those texts against their own cultural and historical backgrounds. Beyond that I will be using Scripture as the benchmark against which I wish my model to be judged. In other words I will go beyond exegesis in order to arrive at my conclusions. I am therefore asking the reader to come on a journey with me, and to respond to my appeal that there needs be an equality of function and status for men and women in the church by the following criterion: 'Is the model biblical, or does it fail because it denies the biblical story'. I will ask that I am not judged simply on whether I have exegeted the Scriptures correctly — if that were the only criterion I am convinced that those who take an opposing viewpoint would not instantly come round to my understanding. Exegesis is important but I believe we must go beyond exegesis and need to hold our model up against Scripture. (The reason for this will become apparent when we come to discuss the issue of slavery and Scripture. Some of our Bible-believing forefathers made significant mistakes on that particular issue.)

To illustrate how we (particularly as charismatics) face a similar problem I will refer the reader to the charismatic understanding and practice of prophecy. It is not possible to prove that current practice is exactly what is being referred to in the New Testament. The amount of material we have on 'congregational prophecy'[2] is so limited — a comment in Thessalonians not to despise prophecy and some corrective Scriptures in Paul's correspondence with the Corinthians. Thus there is minimal material to prove that current practice is identical to the biblical practice. (I also assert that this is even a more acute problem to any non-charismatic who might wish to prove that current practice deviates from New Testament practice — the material being so sparse that it would prove well nigh impossible to critique current charismatic practice in prophecy as being unbiblical. The truth is that we simply cannot be dogmatic.) In the case of spiritual gifts current practice can be held up against Scripture and I believe passionately that current practice actually holds up well. (Such a method is not one where Scripture is strictly exegeted and then practice implemented, rather it is one where a practice is judged against Scripture and if necessary then adjusted in the light of Scripture — similar to the so-called hermeneutical spiral.[3]) This is similar to the methodology that I suggest is best with respect to the issue concerning the place of women in church and society, hence the question raised above: 'Is the model (I am suggesting on women) biblical, or does it fail because it denies the biblical story'.

If I were to take, by way of example, my suggestion that there is very good reason why Jesus chose twelve male apostles (as discussed in

---

[2]By this term I mean prophecy which took place when the congregation assembled together. Thus, by definition, I am excluding OT prophecy and prophetic words such as given by Agabus or ones we find in the book of Revelation. This is not to say that the excluded material is unrelated — far from it, but that we have little material to describe what the content and style of prophetic utterances were in the assembled congregation.

[3]The 'hermeneutical spiral' simply states that we come to Scripture with presuppositions that impact our understanding, but as we read and are 'read' by Scripture our presuppositions change, and thus when we return to Scripture, although we will again come with presuppositions they should be somewhat closer to 'biblical' presuppositions. Thus I am suggesting on many (perhaps all issues / doctrines?) issues that we arrive at a model which Scripture first tests then adjusts.

chapter 3), there is no way that I can prove that my explanation is correct. However, I suggest that the test regarding my suggestion is whether or not it accords well with Scripture, or whether there is another explanation which seems to accord better with the Scriptural story.[4]

I trust as you read the book you will be as challenged as I was in writing it. If your conclusions are different to mine, my only plea is that we continue to respect one another and in our treatment of those who are different to ourselves we learn to relate to them as those who claim to follow Christ.

In writing I acknowledge some of the people who have helped or influenced me greatly. Roger Forster in the mid-1980s first opened my eyes to the possibility of reading the Pauline texts in a more liberating way. The many people I have dialogued with as I have taught on this subject over many years — thank you for the challenging questions. The stimulating writings of Craig Keener, some of which will be referred to in this book. The Pioneer network of churches that have sought, not only to embody what is taught in this book, but also to continue to relate to those who cannot accept these conclusions. Finally, to colleagues and friends who have shown me the acceptance that Christ shows to all, regardless of our status or gender.

My thanks to Peter and Sharon Birch for their friendship and help in publishing this book. Thanks also to Chris Dicken and Sue Erasmus for their help in critiquing the manuscript. Their many helpful comments have made the chapters that follow considerably more

---

[4] This method seems necessary for there is no explicit reason given for the 12 apostles being male. There is no footnote that says, 'and this proves that Jesus would always choose men over women', nor is there a footnote that says, 'but this is not to be taken as a sign that men are favoured over women'. Likewise, there is no Scripture which unequivocally states that women cannot be in leadership, nor one that states that they can. This is not unique to the issue in question, and the comparative discussion on slavery should prove enlightening.

readable. A special thanks must also go to Vivien Culver who gave a lengthy critique of the material. I am most grateful to her scholarly response and am well aware that, in spite of some adjustments, that she would present a different case on numerous points.

In closing this preface I dedicate this book to two people: one female, one male; one whose life has spoken deeply to me, one whose writings and reputation as a follower of Jesus have humbled me. To Christine Noble and Gustavo Gutiérrez I dedicate this book. May we see many more with your spirit rise to lead, provoke, and demonstrate to the church that Jesus is truly the liberator.

For Such A Time As This

CHAPTER 1

BY WHAT AUTHORITY?

The words 'authority' and 'submission' can be very emotive, particularly if we have had a bad experience of someone in authority, or have lived in circumstances that left us disempowered. Gustavo Gutiérrez, among others, has brought us a focus on those who have been disempowered, creatively describing them as those who are absent from our society. In this context he defines 'absent' as those whose presence has been of little or no importance.[1] I write this book as a white, Western male; I must also accept that I am, by global standards, wealthy. I am one of the empowered people, therefore it can be all too easy for me to write about the appropriateness of authority. However, this issue does need to be addressed, but not in order to put people into boxes and into their place, rather in order to help liberate us all to emulate the Jesus we claim to follow.

It seems to me that the very concept of 'authority' has been hijacked and comes across as 'authoritarianism'; likewise the wonderful concept of submission has become enforced subjection. This is a major travesty. Yet there is an opportunity here for the church to model something very different and to speak out against the corrupted use of authority. As far as the exercise of genuine authority is concerned there is a built-in safeguard, given that no-one has authority in themselves; authority is never owned independently. All human authority is derived from God and can only be exercised by his permission and it should go without saying that anyone who exercises authority will have to give an account of how they exercised that authority. God holds accountable all who exercise authority, from the ruler of a nation to the parent in the home.

---

[1] *A Theology of Liberation* (London: SCM, 1988), p. xx.

To be in authority means to have a clear mandate and responsibility to lead, guide and inspire all who should be under that authority. The fact that someone exercises authority does not place them beyond correction — far from it; Jesus reserved his strongest words for those in positions of leadership.

Given the emotive nature of the subject and also the important question that is raised as to the authority that women can exercise I want to take some space to explore the nature of the authority which is approved of by Scripture.[2] I trust that those who find the very words difficult will find a new place of rest in the acceptance and approval of God, and that all those who have the privilege of being 'present' in society or church will submit themselves again to the scrutiny of the exalted one who voluntarily humbled himself and, like him, use their voice to promote all who find themselves 'absent'.

1.   The nature of authority and submission

1.1   Authority — to serve people

Authority that is acceptable to God is so different to the typical Christ-less authoritarianism. Jesus made this clear when he said:

> Jesus called them together and said, "You know that those who are regarded as rulers of the Gentiles lord it over them, and their high officials exercise authority over them. Not so with you. Instead, whoever wants to become great among you must be your servant, and whoever wants to be first must be slave of all. For even the Son of Man did not come to be served, but to

---

[2]There are different types of authority that are appropriate in different situations. Tom Marshall covers three typical categories: that of Task Authority, Teaching Authority and Ethical or Spiritual Authority. I will not be examining authority along these categories, rather I want to examine the attitudes that are appropriate in those with authority. I suggest that Marshall's book, *Understanding Leadership* (Chichester: Sovereign World, 1991), be consulted, particularly pp. 42-113.

serve, and to give his life as a ransom for many." (Mark 10:42-
45).

In Christ, our authority is not over people, but to serve them. So Paul
says in 2 Corinthians 13:10 that his authority was to build the church up
— to promote them rather than 'lord it' over them. Likewise Peter
exhorts elders to serve the flock, not by 'lording it' over them, but by
being examples to them (1 Peter 5:1-4). Leadership can abuse authority
through 'lording it' over people but this is removed from the spirit of
Christ. We can safely say that any authority that tries to dominate or
intimidate people is an illegitimate authority as far as Scripture is
concerned.

1.2   Authority — over the works of the devil

One example of the authority that Jesus gives to his disciples is found in
Luke 10:19 where he says:

> I have given you authority to trample on snakes and scorpions
> and to overcome all the power of the enemy; nothing will harm
> you.

Christ wishes to give us authority over the enemies that seek to bring
people into bondage. Such authority will more effectively help us serve
other people. Although we live with the tension of the 'already' but 'not
yet' of the presence of God's kingdom, perhaps we will see more
effective authority over the devil in our communities when there is a
greater desire to emulate Jesus who laid down his life for others. It is
certainly important that we do not end up seeking to exercise a wrong
authority over people, for then we will find that we have been serving the
devil.

1.3   Authority — flows from being in submission

Luke 7:1-10 records the story of the centurion who recognised that
Jesus moved in authority because, like himself, he was submitted to
authority.

If we desire to exercise legitimate authority in a Christ-like way, then we too need to ensure that we are those people who are ourselves under authority. There are no hierarchies where we can get to the top of the pyramid and so reach a position where we do not need to be under authority. Ultimately we are all under God's authority, but this is 'made flesh' as we submit to the spirit of Christ which is revealed in his people, the church. Paul[3] says that we are to, 'Submit to one another out of reverence for Christ' (Ephesians 5:21). The importance of this principle will become self-evident under this next heading.

1.4   Submission — a command for all believers

Nowhere are those in authority told to 'subject' those who are 'under' them. Rather submission is a voluntary response that is commanded by God.[4] We are to serve others, not subject them. Regardless of the position or title we hold, we are to ensure that in attitude we are submissive. There is no believer that is exempt from the need to display this submissive attitude. Although equality might be a myth, any concept of hierarchical power is repugnant to the spirit of the gospel which comes to release all believers into servanthood.

Effectively this means that I cannot claim that my position (within church, society, marriage or family) exempts me from submission. I cannot claim, on the basis of a verse of Scripture that says, 'Wives, submit to your husbands' (Ephesians 5:22), that I therefore should not submit to my wife. If I am to be a follower of Jesus it is also required that I too am submissive.[5] Indeed it can be argued that the more authority a person has been mandated to exercise that an equally greater level of submission must be demonstrated.

---

[3]Although some scholars question whether Paul was the author of Ephesians, for the purposes of this book I will use the term 'Paul' or 'Pauline' of all the books that have been traditionally credited to him, that is Romans to Philemon.

[4]The Greek 'voice' used is consistently the middle one, which must be translated as 'submit yourselves'.

[5]We will examine later the concept of authority within marriage.

1.5 Conclusions on the nature of authority and submission

We conclude that no-one is allowed to lord it over others, nor is anyone allowed to be insubmissive in heart. This conclusion has an important bearing on the issue of women and authority. It means that questions such as 'can a woman have authority over a man?' is an inappropriate question. In that emotive sense, it is also inappropriate for a man to have authority over a woman. When authority is exercised in a Christ-like way the legitimate question will rather become, 'what level of authority can a woman have to serve others?'.

2. Realms of authority

All authority resides in God. However, he has delegated some of that authority into the human sphere.[6] Understanding that no person is ever in a position of absolute authority, thereby being able to demand absolute obedience from us, should help take some of the 'sting' out of the concept of authority.

The distinct spheres of authority that we can define are as follows:[7]

1. God

2. Scripture

3. Conscience

4. Government

5. Employer

6. Church

7. Marriage and family

---

[6] The human spheres that are of particular interest on the subject of women in leadership are enumerated in Scripture in what is known as the 'Household Codes'. These codes will be looked at in more detail in chapter 4

[7] I acknowledge that it might well be possible to list these differently.

Within these seven spheres I wish to make the further three distinctions to show that not all seven spheres are at the same 'level' of authority:

2.1 Absolute authority — total obedience

The first two spheres (God and Scripture) are absolute and can consequently demand absolute obedience. Disobedience to God or to what he says can only be described as rebellion. Only God carries such an authority and we are to submit to Scripture for in doing so we are submitting to God. We obviously need to interpret Scripture and determine how its teachings should be applied (as we are seeking to do in this book on the specific subject of women) but we cannot ignore its teachings.

2.2 Relative authority — not to be violated

The conscience is not an infallible guide, but we are to keep our conscience clear (Acts 24:16). We violate our conscience to our peril, thus holding on to our personal convictions as to what it means to obey God must be given a higher priority than simply obeying a human edict (Acts 5:29). Likewise should we be in a position of authority and use that position to violate someone else's conscience we would be stepping beyond the legitimate exercise of our authority.

The conscience, however, is not an absolute authority for it is conditioned through culture, upbringing, personality and experience. The conscience needs educating and therefore needs exposure to the Holy Spirit, to Scripture and to those who can bring wise counsel. This means that we cannot elevate the conscience to a position of absolute authority in our lives, yet this does not negate the importance of understanding that no human authority can demand that we do something that would cause us to go against our own conscience.

This latter point will become increasingly important to grasp as we examine the nature of the remaining spheres of authority.

2.3 Delegated human authority

The exercise of authority in these final four spheres of government, employer, church and family, is to be seen as delegated authority — therefore the ones in authority have to answer to God for how they exercised their authority. I suggest that the 'level' of authority within these spheres is lower than that of the first three we have looked at. We do not encounter an absolute level of authority that can demand unconditional obedience, nor do we encounter a level of authority that means that we can ignore our conscience. As these four spheres are significantly related to one another, in the sense that they cover four aspects of human relationships, it will be helpful to outline some of the specific characteristics in more detail.

2.3.1 Independence of spheres

These four spheres each cover an independent aspect of human life and relationships and are independent of one another. This means that someone in authority in one sphere is not automatically in authority in another, and cannot simply transfer their authority to another sphere. For instance, someone in authority at work is not automatically in authority in the church.

However, there is a mutual appeal to the truth which needs to be an influence on those in authority. If we take the example of a person at work who now comes into the church sphere, we will see how this works out. If this person is unhappy about some aspect of church life she could appeal to the truth and ask that those in authority in the church reconsider what they are doing. She cannot, however, come and legislate what is done, as this is not her sphere of authority. Conversely if one of the church leaders is employed by this person, that church leader cannot dictate the terms by which he will work for her. The spheres remain independent, so that to be in authority in one sphere does not automatically make a person in authority in another.

2.3.2 Cannot demand absolute obedience

Absolute obedience cannot be required by any of these authorities —
that right belongs only to God. Each person will give an account for their
own behaviour (Romans 14:10-12). A person 'under' authority cannot
blame someone in authority for instructing them to do something
immoral. In examining these types of authority it is important to note that
no other person can demand absolute obedience from us: this applies
right across the spectrum, from the government to the interpersonal
relationships within the family or church. (Obviously disobedience to a
request / command might well have consequences ranging from
imprisonment to a loss of friendship.)

2.3.3 Do we submit to the person or what they represent?

As far as women operating within these spheres, there is a significant
issue to face for those who object to a woman in a place of authority. If
it is wrong for a woman to exercise any authority over a man, when
does it become wrong and in what sphere(s) is it wrong? Is it only
wrong in the church sphere or is it also wrong in the work sphere? Or is
it also wrong for a woman to be an MP or to take on the position of
Prime Minister? And for the royalists — is it wrong for males within a
nation to acknowledge a female monarch?

We would all agree that it is certainly not wrong for a mother to
discipline a son! Does it then become wrong when the son has become
an adult and has left home — and if so has it become wrong because of
the male / female aspect or because the relationship has moved to a new
stage irrespective of gender issues? However, somewhat more
poignantly, I would like to ask whether or not it is right for a
policewoman to insist on a male driver stopping when he is speeding? If
it is genuinely wrong for a woman to exercise authority, the male (and let
us assume he is a 'Bible-believing' Christian male) must surely be left
with the following dilemma: does he stop in order to fulfil the (biblical)

requirement of submitting to governing authorities or does he carry on so as he does not submit to a woman?

Those who object to women in leadership will almost certainly respond (rightly, I might add) with the observation that the issue is not of submitting to a woman but to what she represents, that is the government. This illustration raises a very important aspect, namely that with delegated human authorities we are not so much submitting to the person, but to what they represent. Surely the situation within the church is not too dissimilar: we do not submit to a male leader because he is male, but because of what he represents.[8] If we insist on male leadership we need to be careful that we have not elevated maleness over who leadership represents. If women in leadership is wrong then a more consistent response would be to suggest it is wrong in every sphere unless it can be clearly shown that it is only restricted within the church (and perhaps family) sphere.

This issue (along with many others) is wrestled with in the book *Recovering Biblical Manhood and Womanhood.*[9] The way it is dealt with seems to me to indicate the very real problem faced by those who want to deny women any type of authority. A few examples are given below.

The authors claim that women can be involved in 'unofficial' guidance, as was the case with Priscilla, but not as part of an 'official' teaching leadership. They acknowledge that there are 'ambiguities' but that the underlying principles of the appropriate roles for men and women must be maintained.[10] This begs the question as to what the underlying principles are. For these authors it is that of maintaining male leadership, yet surely the inconsistency is there for all to read when they

---

[8]We will of course have to look at the Scriptures that might limit any leadership role within the church to males in due course.
[9](Wheaton: Crossway, 1991) edited by John Piper and Wayne Grudem.
[10]Ibid., p. 85.

15

say, 'For the sake of finishing the Great Commission in our day, we are willing to risk some less-than-ideal role assignments'.[11] Are these assignments less-than-ideal or simply unbiblical? Surely they cannot have it both ways.

I find it interesting that they do not insist upon women being subordinate in society. If creation-order states that women are subordinate then this must apply to all people in every aspect of creation, not simply within the church.[12] They do however hint that in society there are certain roles that are not suitable for women. A female umpire would be inappropriate to settle heated disputes among men. This is not due to male egotism, but to 'a natural and good penchant given by God'![13] Perhaps I lack in faith but am totally unconvinced by such arguments! It totally eludes me as to how the above illustration has any bearing at all on the key issue of church leadership, for surely as those who are renewed by the Spirit we are exhorted to respond to truth in a submissive attitude and not in a way that demonstrates male (or female) egos. Disputes are not resolved because some 'strong' male can enforce a decision — they are resolved by hearing what the Spirit has to say through Scripture in the context of the body.

They suggest that a mature woman who is in leadership will, of course, 'affirm and receive and nurture the strength and leadership of men *in some form*'.[14] Examples are then given of women in leadership with an explanation that they will relate differently than males would to those under them. Apparently, for example, a female bus driver will relate differently to her passengers than a male bus driver for she will

---

[11]Ibid., pp. 76f.

[12]Ironically if there was one sphere that should be exempt from an ordering of relationships based upon a 'creation-order' it should be the church. The church participates in the new creation, society in the created-order.

[13] *Manhood*, p. 52.

[14]Ibid., p. 50. (Italics original.)

fulfil her leadership role in a way that 'signals to men her endorsement of their responsibility to lead'.

In all of their discussion the guidance over what is appropriate for a woman in relationship to leadership is over the issue of how directive and personal the leadership is. Apparently the more personal the interaction, the more inappropriate it is for them to exert directive influence.[15] If this is so then, given the model of leadership in most churches (distant and official, not personal and relational), it would seem that a woman occupying a position of leadership within many churches should not be an issue at all!

It seems to me that arguments such as given above miss the essential element that we are all required to submit to what is right and true: effectively we submit to God through his delegated authority. To argue as Piper and Grudem do above is to elevate the person that we are submitting to, rather than the authority that they represent.

2.3.4 Two emotive illustrations of the independence of the spheres

Unless we have taken the extreme position that women can never exercise any position of authority in any sphere, we can agree with the illustration I gave above of a person at work not automatically being in authority within the church and vice versa. A church leader employed by a church member would be requested to submit to the employer, while the employer would be expected to follow the leadership given by the church leader. Provided that neither party is seeking to 'lord it over' the other party they would then seek to respect the distinctive nature of the spheres, and operate within those parameters appropriately.

I wish to examine later the issue of leadership within marriage, but for the sake of the following two illustrations I would like us to assume that Scripture teaches marriage in such a way that the husband is

---

[15]Ibid., p. 51.

the one in authority. Let us now make the illustration of the independence of the spheres a little more emotive!

Suppose a husband and wife both work for the same company. We will make the wife occupy a senior position to the husband and that he is directly responsible to her. It follows that in the work scenario he would submit to her as his 'boss', but at home she would submit to him as her husband.[16]

If our understanding of authority is that we can obtain a position that means we can dictate to others what they should do, we will always struggle with the illustration above and in particular the one that follows. However, if we understand that authority is there to release those we are responsible for into their freedom we will see how challenging and rewarding the exercise of true authority is.

Now let's make our illustration even more emotive (and indeed extreme) yet. If we accept, for the sake of our current illustration, that the wife is to submit to her husband in the marriage sphere and that the husband's leadership role means that he is to lead her to discover the gifts and call of God within her. Let us then assume that in fellowship with others it is clear that she has a gift of leadership that should be outworked in the church sphere, while his role is elsewhere.[17] How then would we outwork such a scenario? If authority means that we can insist on our own way the marriage would soon be in difficulties! The husband would make life difficult at home while the wife would look to reverse the situation in church!

---

[16]I am well aware that I am drawing a very artificial line between husband and wife, they are one flesh in partnership together. I am simply making the illustration and model of marriage extreme to show the reality of the independence of the spheres.
[17]We have made this illustration in the extreme form. In reality given that husbands and wives are a team it is unlikely that the two would be operating in totally different spheres.

Once we understand the purpose of authority is to release us to serve one another, we can begin to model the harmonious relationships we see within the Trinity. Such relationships need to be modelled within the church. The example in the previous paragraph would be a true illustration of submission to one another, only made possible by being truly filled with the Spirit of Christ (Ephesians 5:18-21).[18] The illustration, as given, is an extreme one — we face none of the potential conflicts if the women released were single or the married couple were released together. However, even the most extreme situation is made possible through the radical liberation the gospel brings — a liberation for women and a liberation for everyone from insecurity and inordinate self-protection.

2.4   Do all women need to submit to men?

I propose to look at biblical principles that can operate within marriage later, but would like to address one important question here. This question will relate to the possibility of women being in leadership. Again I am assuming (although I will seek to bring qualification to that position in due course) that there is an order within marriage of wives submitting to husbands, but want to address the possibility of all women needing to submit to men. If this were so, we would have discovered a significant block on them exercising any position of authority within the church (and logically, as indicated above, within any aspect of society).

If it were true that all women must submit to all men, we would be dealing with a very big truth. We would be faced with an immutable law, a universal ordering of things based on gender alone. Women would have to submit because they are female and men would rule because they are male. For those who have a high view of Scripture we would never expect to find a single approving instance of a woman

---

[18]The underlying basis for submission is being filled with the Spirit. This makes possible mutual edification and mutual submission. Without a yielding to the Spirit there will always be the tendency to demand that others bow to our will.

exercising authority. (Later we will see some of those 'unexpected' instances.) If an immutable law were in force, it would be at least as clearly and definitely stated as any of the other principles of God's will.

Some have suggested that all women need to be in submission to all men and this position is often taken to include single women thus making it a universal principle. Regardless of one's understanding of the term 'head' and the call for wives to submit to their husbands, to press this to include a blanket 'headship' of men over women and a universal requirement of women to submit to men, is to go far beyond the New Testament position.

There are specific Scriptures which can be used to suggest that wives should be submissive to their *own* husbands.[19] This is made explicit with the Greek phrase: *tois idiois andrasin* — 'to their own husbands'. In other words these Scriptures do not teach that all women are to submit to all men, or to all married men — but that wives are to submit to their own husbands. The submission is limited to the marriage relationship.

The only relevant Scripture remaining is 1 Corinthians 11:3 which reads in the NIV as, 'And the head of the woman is man'. This translation could suggest that Paul is outlining a universal principle of the headship of men over women. However there are reasons why this is not what he intends us to understand:

First, Paul explicitly says of the male that 'the head of every man is Christ' but does not repeat the word *every* when he addresses the situation with women. He does not state 'the head of *every* woman...'[20]

---

[19] 1 Cor. 14:34f., Ephes. 5:22, Tit. 2:5 and 1 Pet. 3:1. In Col. 3:18 Paul does not add the specific term *own* husbands but from the context there is no dispute that is indeed what he is stating.

[20] Even if he had done so we would still have to determine whether he meant every woman or every married woman, as the Greek word used here for woman, *gune*, can mean either, and in the context here probably means the latter.

Secondly, the NIV translation chooses to translate the Greek in a most definitive way. The Greek text has a definite article (the word 'the') with the word 'man' but no definite article with the word 'woman'. Thus the text could easily read 'the head of a woman is *the* man', so indicating that the woman's head is the specific man that is in relationship to her, i.e. her own husband.[21]

(We also should note that even if Paul was intending to indicate some universal headship of men in relation to women that there is, as yet, no total agreement as to the meaning of the word head (*kephale*). If this word was to mean 'source' and his appeal to creation was being used to illustrate this truth, there would then be no indication within this passage of anything approaching the necessity of all women being in submission to men.) We therefore conclude that nowhere does Scripture teach the universal submission of all women to men. Thus when we discover in Scripture women exercising authority in a Christ-like spirit we do not detect any disapproval of such a situation.

Women — by what authority?

Once we understand authority along the lines outlined above we have immediately removed a large objection to women in leadership. It is clear that a woman who exercises an authority which dictates over a man is exercising an illegitimate authority, but neither can a man exercise such an authority legitimately. The issue is not whether a woman can exercise an authority *over* another person — rather the question that

---

[21]J. Armitage Robinson translates this as 'a woman's head is her husband' in *St. Paul's Epistle to the Ephesians* (London: Macmillan & Co., 1993), p. 205. Robertson and Plummer's commentary in the ICC series gives the same translation (Edinburgh: T & T Clark, 1971) p. 227. Cf. also NRSV: 'the husband is the head of his wife'. Likewise, E. Earle Ellis in, *Pauline Theology-Ministry and Society* (Grand Rapids: Eerdmans; Exeter: Paternoster, 1989), pp. 59f., translates this as 'the head of every husband is Christ, the head of the wife is the husband, and the head of Christ is God ...the husband (exists as) the image and glory of God, but the wife is the glory of the husband' (1 Cor. 11:3,7).

remains is whether a woman can have the same rights as a man to lay down her life in service of others. Obviously we will need to examine any Scriptures that might seem to limit the role of leadership to men, but prior to that I suggest that we explore next how our understanding of the nature of church might help lead us to certain conclusions.

CHAPTER 2

LEADING IN THE CHURCH: WHICH CHURCH?

We all know that the church is not the building but is constituted by the people. Yet this by itself is an inadequate definition and one which needs to be qualified and expanded. The way in which we define the nature of church will in part determine how we approach the issue of women in relationship to leadership within the church.

In *The Household of God*[1] Lesslie Newbigin suggested that the 'Church Universal' was made up of three distinct traditions. Each tradition having a distinctive approach to church which is then reflected in their respective practices and beliefs. The three traditions that Newbigin discerned were that of the Catholic, Protestant and Pentecostal traditions. Although there would be considerable dispute as to whether all Pentecostals are distinct from the Protestant tradition,[2] the three strands do highlight in broad terms the distinctive ecclesiological bases from which the traditions develop.[3] The definitions, although not

---

[1](London: SCM, 1953 / New York: Friendship, 1954).

[2]Consider the critique of the North American Assemblies of God by Margaret Poloma in *The Assemblies of God at the Crossroads: Charisma and Institutional Dilemmas* (Knoxville: University of Tennessee, 1989). Its institutionalism suggested to her that this Pentecostal denomination was no longer displaying a distinct tradition. Harvey Cox in *Fire from Heaven* (Reading, MA: Addison-Wesley, 1994), suggests something very similar. James McClendon Jr. in *Systematic Theology*, Vol. 2 (Nashville: Abingdon, 1994), suggests that Newbigin's third strand owed 'more to the book of Acts than to any firsthand knowledge' (p. 342).

[3]These three traditions are utilised by Wally Fahrer, *Building on the Rock* (Scottdale: Herald, 1995). The third tradition for him is that of the Anabaptist-Mennonite. Others, including myself, like to call this third tradition the Pneumatic tradition.

watertight, indicate which factor (sacrament, word or Spirit respectively)[4] is understood as central to bringing definition to the nature of church.

Dependent on which tradition is identified with will in part determine the questions that need to be answered with respect to the appropriateness of women in leadership. In what follows, I will try to highlight, as far as possible without bias, the distinctive bases to the traditions and the resultant central issue on the women in leadership question.

1.   The Sacramental — Catholic tradition

Those within this tradition see the church as an institution. The church being instituted through Christ who in turn appointed Peter as the rock upon which the church is built. No-one has the right to change the nature of church as it is not a human invention nor creation. Apostolic succession becomes important, and a greater weight can therefore be placed upon tradition which is seen as the teaching of the church that Jesus initiated.

With regard to the offices in the church, this model outworks at a localised level in the person of the priest or vicar ('vicar' essentially being another term for priest: one who represents another party). The priest represents Christ and has a very specific role in administering the appointed means of grace (the sacraments) to the people. Should one participate in this Jesus-ordained church, by following its teachings and receiving the sacraments by the appointed personnel, then one can be assured of salvation. (Perhaps there is a danger that this could deteriorate into a greater faith in the institution for salvation than in Christ.)

The 'furniture' within such a tradition also tells a story: the altar is placed centre-stage as the service leads up to the high point of the

---

[4]These factors could equally be defined as order, faith and experience.

Eucharist or Mass. Under such a model of church, the question that is provoked regarding women is that of determining whether a woman can be a priest. In other words can a woman represent a (male) Messiah?

2.   The Word — Protestant tradition

The Protestant Reformation gave us the revelation of justification by faith and the desire to give the Bible back to the people. These two key contributions caused a radical redefinition of church. Church was no longer to be defined historically through apostolic succession, but on the basis of those who had submitted to the truth. The key element that is thereby elevated is a right understanding and response to teaching, rather than accepting the church as an institution. (At worst, of course, such a view could deteriorate into simple mental assent to doctrine.)

The priest was no longer necessary (and indeed by some was believed to be unbiblical) as all believers were priests to God. However, the importance of right teaching and therefore accurate belief meant that there was now the need for a capable minister of the word, which would normally demand that he (and it was usually a 'he') was theologically trained. Maturity was not to come through a regular participation in the sacraments but through a growth of understanding, as it is submission to the truth that sets people free.

The altar, under this model, is no longer central, rather it is the pulpit that takes over the central focus. The worship does not lead to the sacraments but rather to the ministry of the word as we are not fed by the Eucharist, but by the word.[5] Going to church becomes an important element with buildings and set times being a means by which church is

---

[5]It can be argued that for some of the Protestant groups the preaching of the word has become another sacrament. McClendon (a Baptist with an Anabaptist approach) suggests that there are three main 'remembering signs': that of baptism, the Lord's Supper and of 'prophetic preaching' *(Systematic Theology,* Vol. 2, pp. 386-402). In this he is following in the neo-orthodox tradition of Barth, et al.

expressed. Statements of faith are often an essential part of this tradition in order to draw the boundaries around a group; those who can subscribe to such beliefs are in and those who cannot are out.

Again this tradition raises a question that has to be answered with regard to the position of women within their church setting. It is the inevitable question of the appropriateness of women giving authoritative teaching and so the Timothy passage[6] that seems to restrict this role to men, is seen as a central passage that needs addressing.

3.   The Pneumatic — Pentecostal tradition

This is the tradition that Newbigin called 'Pentecostal' and we might want to call 'Charismatic', however it is probably better called 'Pneumatic' so that we do not simply think of charismatic gifts such as healing, tongues etc. as being the determining factor. Throughout history there have always been the radicals who have tended to be charismatic in the sense that they want to be led, and constituted as church, by the Spirit's activity and presence among them.[7] All three traditions suggest that the church is divinely constituted, but the distinctive claim of the third strand is that it is the recognisable presence of the Spirit in power that determines where the church is.[8] Although there might be considerable dispute as to how we discern where the Spirit is present,[9] if it is the Spirit that defines the New Testament people it is then argued that it

---

[6]1 Tim. 2:11-15 with the key phrase being verse 12 and Paul's words that he did 'not allow a woman to teach...'

[7]See for instance, Donald Durnbaugh, *The Believers' Church* (New York: Macmillan, 1968 / Scottdale: Herald Press, 1985); or less academic and with a strong Pentecostal bias, Eddie Hyatt, *2000 Years of Charismatic Christianity* (Tulsa / Chicota: Hyatt International Ministries, 1996).

[8]Newbigin, *Household*, 94f.

[9]Witness the debate of the mid 1990's that resulted from the 'Toronto Blessing'.

must be that same Spirit who defines a specific people as 'church'; the earthly manifestation of the heavenly gathering around the risen Christ.[10]

From this perspective of the Spirit (and not just the gift of the Spirit as a personal and private experience) as the boundary marker for the New Testament people of God, the terminology of going to church then becomes unacceptable language. It is argued that the New Testament did not subscribe to the understanding that they 'went to church', but rather that their relationships together defined them as church, and when they assembled they assembled *as* church. Such corporate gatherings were designed to enhance their life together (1 Cor. 11:17f.) but the meetings themselves did not constitute them as church. Obviously there is New Testament evidence that the church assembled together and that it was encouraged to continue to do so for mutual edification, but the thrust of the New Testament means that

---

[10]The latter part of this sentence raises a number of issues that need expanding. There is a significant move to understand the gift of the Spirit as the NT counterpart to the OT gift of the law to Israel. The law gave identity to Israel and served as a boundary marker. From a NT perspective it is the gift of the Spirit that serves those purposes for the church, so that 'those who are led by the Spirit are the children of God' (Rom. 8:14, I have adjusted the NIV translation from 'sons' to 'children' to read inclusively). The presence of the Spirit then defines both the church and a specific body of people as church. We see this in the book of Acts in the situation with Cornelius' household. They are included into the community of God when they exhibited the manifest presence of the Spirit. Those who were formerly 'unclean' had passed the test (Acts 15:9) and therefore could not be refused baptism.

The definition of church as an earthly manifestation of the heavenly gathering is from P.T. O'Brien's article 'Church' in *Dictionary of Paul and his Letters* (Downers Grove: IVP, 1993). He suggests that the local churches are not to be seen primarily as components of some world-wide earthly church, but as full manifestations in time and space of the one true heavenly eschatological assembly. This is an important perspective and also has bearing on the issue of women and their role. The church is called to model the relational dynamic of the new creation, and not simply to accommodate itself to relational restrictions that might be found in the creation-order.

corporate meetings themselves should not be considered as being what defines a people as church.

As far as women having a part to play within this tradition, there is only one key question to be answered: it is the question of discerning who it is that God has anointed, and as this anointing transcends racial, social and gender boundaries, there should be no restriction placed on women. It is interesting to note that within many Pentecostal / Charismatic / revival situations that women have a much greater role than in other situations.[11] Pneumatics would wish to ensure that nothing was elevated above the anointing as the evidence of God's choice; gender could not be a higher criterion than the gifting of God's Spirit. The issue to be faced then is whether or not women can be anointed to the same extent as men and lead by example, so requesting that others follow them as they follow Christ.

For those who embrace such a tradition, not only will the issue of anointing be applicable with respect to women, but it should be brought into focus with respect to all those who participate within such a body. Faithfulness to this tradition should mean that the church cannot simply operate from pre-set agendas but according to anointed people and their corresponding burdens. (As with each of the traditions there is a potential weakness; the weakness of this tradition becoming evident when an individual claims the anointing of the Spirit as the reason for their particular behaviour and leading.)

---

[11]Chris Cartwright in a paper presented to a Pentecostal Conference, 'The Role of Women in the Government of the Church', notes that as the Elim Pentecostal Movement developed (institutionalised?) they moved away from the ordination of women. So from the early days 'Elim has had women ministers of prominence and distinction', but since 1929 when ordination was introduced, Elim has not ordained them, thus once official ordination was brought in women were demoted (pp. 11f.). See also the article by John Christopher Thomas 'Women, Pentecostals and the Bible: An Experiment in Pentecostal Hermeneutics' in a *Journal of Pentecostal Theology*, Issue 5, (October 1994), pp. 41-56. This aspect will also be picked up in an Appendix of this book.

The following table will seek to draw out the distinctive elements that come through in each tradition:

	Sacramental	Protestant	Pneumatic
Constituted by:	Apostolic succession	Word / belief	Presence of Spirit
Administered by:	Priests	Ministers of word	Anointed leaders
Denoted by:	Altar	Pulpit	God's Presence
Women:	Can they represent Christ who was male?	Can they teach with authority?	Can they be equally anointed?

By so dividing the three traditions, it is important to note that they are not watertight compartments, but indicate that the central defining factor (sacrament / word / Spirit) is what gives the particular distinctive.

4.   The Church and Women

As I sit firmly within the Pneumatic tradition, I want to highlight that there should be the least objection to women functioning alongside men coming from this camp. However as a Pneumatic tradition would also want to give significant weight to the teachings of Scripture, an evident anointing of the Spirit in and of itself will not be a sufficient answer. Scripture will have to be examined, but the teaching of Scripture on the hallmarks of the outpouring of the Spirit will be a major key. So the effects of the outpouring of the Spirit in Acts 2, which includes an outpouring of the Spirit on all marginalised groups — young, old, women and slaves — would be a major shaping element in understanding the appropriate role for women within the Christian community.[12]

---

[12]Jürgen Moltmann is provocative when he asks the question in relation to Acts 2, 'Does a Christian church that shuts women out from preaching and prophesying have the Holy Spirit, or does such exclusion 'dampen' the Spirit and suppress the Spirit's free work?' (From p. 14 of his article 'A Pentecostal Theology of Life' in *Journal of Pentecostal Theology*, Issue 9, (October 1996).)

For the Protestant tradition, any biblical restrictions on roles for women will be of great importance. However the presence of missiological and other factors within any restrictive passages will have to be given due weight. So the application of hermeneutical principles[13] will be a key factor in discovering not simply *what* the Bible says, but *why* it says what it does and *how* that should be applied today.

I also have a great appreciation for the Sacramental approach with its seeming emphasis on transcendence, but in all honesty I am probably the furthest away from this particular tradition. The question(s) that this tradition asks of itself regarding a suitable role for women is best left to those who write from within this perspective. However, I would want to raise the following three points for consideration:

1) How essential is it that Christ was male for him to act as the representative of God?, and consequently how essential is gender for the people who represent Christ?[14]

2) There is a strong tendency within the sacramental tradition to talk of the church as the 'mother church'. Perhaps this imagery could be explored to suggest that there could be an appropriateness in the motherly function and identity of the church no longer being focused exclusively in a male priesthood.[15]

3) Further, if an ordained priesthood is believed in, this cannot be at the expense of the priesthood of all believers. Indeed, perhaps the idea of a

---

[13]'Hermeneutics' is the overall heading for the methods used to interpret Scripture.

[14]The material in Chapter 8 on the maleness of Christ might be of particular interest for the Sacramental tradition.

[15]Miroslav Volf, After Our Likeness: The Church as the Image of the Trinity (Grand Rapids: Eerdmans, 1998), p. 165, makes this point. Volf makes reference to an article by Hervé-Marie Legrand, 'Traditio perpetue servate? The Non-ordination of Women: Tradition or Simply an Historical Fact?' in Worship 65 (1991), pp. 428-508, who maintains that even the Catholic tradition does not contain any strictly dogmatic reasons proscribing the ordination of women.

clergy is not so much the problem as the corresponding idea of a laity. Perhaps a move forward would be to abandon the concept of the laity, or at least to blur the line between clergy and laity with the clergy seen more as appointed representatives of the wider body of people rather than as representative of the male Messiah. There could well be a need for those within this tradition to recover some of the 'raw' beginnings of the faith and express more of that within their tradition. Vincent Branick, a Catholic writer, astutely observes the change from the Pauline model to that of the later church with the words that:

> A clergy developed — or more precisely a laity developed. Formal patterns of assembly and formal seating arrangements arose... The church sought to reappropriate the cult of the Old Testament. The community sought a temple with an altar. Perhaps we have here an irrepressible quest for holy place.

> At a meeting sometime between AD 360 and 370, a synod of Laodicea forbade the holding of Eucharist in the home: ...The prohibition of Laodicea completes a critical cycle. The Lord's Supper had changed from evening meal to stylized ritual. The assembly had moved from dining room to sacred hall. Leadership had shifted from family members to special clergy. Now the original form of church was declared illegal.[16]

Regardless of the tradition that one identifies with, I believe that all church traditions need to take note of the words of Thomas Finger:

> Ecclesiology has often been one of theology's least innovative and interesting loci. Systematic theology has often served well-

---

[16]*The House Church in the Writings of Paul* (Wilmington, DE: Michael Glazier, 1989), 133f. This was the same council that, at least by some interpretations, banned women from being elders. Branick's bold criticism needs to be made by all people within their respective traditions, otherwise it might not simply be the Catholic tradition that runs the risk of declaring the original form of church as illegal!

established institutions, and rigidified and legitimized their doctrines and practices. Rather than inquiring afresh into the church's nature and its mission in the world, theologians have sometimes been more anxious to defend those structures which paid their salaries.[17]

Perhaps it is time to re-examine the basis of church so as we ask the penetrating question as to why we do what we do. If we cannot find an answer that satisfies it might indicate that it is time to explore new ways of being church together. As we do so the place of women within church should be looked at from new angles. My personal plea, as someone within the Pneumatic tradition, to those who identify with other traditions would be to give greater consideration to the anointing of the Spirit as the means of identifying leadership.

Once the Spirit was outpoured on Cornelius' household, Peter responded with the pragmatic (or spiritually discerning?) rhetorical question: 'Can anyone keep these people from being baptised with water?' (Acts 10:47). In a similar way if the Spirit has been outpoured as in Acts 2 upon all flesh, should we not also ask a corresponding question when it is evident that the person anointed by the Spirit is a woman? In such a situation our question then would be: 'Can anyone keep this woman from fulfilling the reason why God has anointed her?'.[18]

---

[17]Finger, *Christian Theology*, Vol. 2 (Scottdale: Herald, 1989), 225f. Finger's comments are not to be limited to theologians, and the term 'salary' could be extended to include position, authority, esteem, honour etc.

[18]I am aware that there are those who distinguish between the anointing of the Spirit for ministry (open to all) and an anointing for leadership in a 'governmental' sense (restricted to men). As this book progresses this issue will be addressed. At this stage I am raising the issue of anointing and the less formal or institutionalised our view of church is the easier the acceptance of women functioning in an unrestricted way should be.

Closely aligned to the nature of church is its mission. Indeed it can be argued that there is more material on the mission of the church in the New Testament than on its actual shape and structure. So it is important that, in any age and society, the church is shaped appropriately in order to fulfil its mission, and in chapter 4 we will examine the presence of missiological principles within the New Testament that in part shaped the place of women within those churches. Prior to this, however, we will next give an overview of the place of women within the Bible.

For Such A Time As This

CHAPTER 3

WOMEN AND WOMAN IN THE BIBLE

In this chapter I intend to sketch the response to women that is found in Scripture. After considering the Old Testament material I will focus mainly on the response by Jesus and Paul to women. The former because he is not simply the founder of our faith but is *the* 'image of God',[1] which has enormous repercussions for our hermeneutical approach to Scripture. If Jesus, in the entirety of his redemptive life and death, is the revelation of God then we must give him centre place hermeneutically. We cannot afford to sideline his life and actions, but need to see them as revealing God to us; in the words of Norman Kraus, Jesus must be the 'hermeneutical norm for biblical revelation'.[2] What he said and did must help shape our thinking regarding the overall biblical material on women. Paul is given significant space too because of his prominence in the New Testament, and also because of the accusation that is labelled against him that we find in his letters, the 'most strikingly antifeminist passages' of the New Testament.[3]

1. The Old Testament material

The first two chapters of Genesis are key in discovering how things were 'in the beginning'. Jesus used this principle when discussing the thorny issue of divorce and remarriage which suggests that the creation narratives indicate norms for a God-ordered society. Chapters 3-11 of Genesis indicate what has gone wrong, and in the context of our study

---

[1]See e.g. 2 Cor. 4:4; Col. 1:15; Heb. 1:3.
[2]*God our Savior* (Scottdale: Herald Press, 1991), p. 51.
[3]Mary Daly, *The Church and the Second Sex* (New York: Harper & Row, 1968), p. 38. The specific texts that might seem to restrict women will be looked at in chapter 6.

chapter 3 is key. The remainder of the Old Testament then outlines the ordering of life within Israel. Having completed this material on beginnings, fall and life within Israel, we will be ready to examine the arrival of Jesus and his response to women.

1.1 Creation narratives

There are two accounts of creation and in the first account (Genesis 1:26-28) we have the simple revelation that humanity consists of males and females made in the image of God. Undoubtedly there is a relational element in this statement with men and women *together* being in the image of God, but for our purposes it is clear that there is no indication of any inequality. We do not read that men are in the image of God and women are in the image of men, but that humanity, both male and female together, are in the image of God. Of equal significance is the fact that the commission to rule is given to both of them ('let *them* rule' - Genesis 1:26) without any indication of what would be an appropriate female or male role. In this first chapter we find no indication of inferiority.

In chapter 2 we have the second account of creation with an introduction to Adam as male[4] and to his wife Eve. It is this second account of creation that is used to teach that there was a clear subordination of the wife to the husband; some even go further suggesting a subordination of all women to men.

Although there will be general principles taught here about the interrelationship of men and women, this chapter is addressing the specific case of a married couple. So even if there is a subordination taught in this chapter we would need to exercise great caution in extending this beyond the marriage relationship.

---

[4]In chapter 1 the term 'Adam' has been used for humanity incorporating male and female as the Hebrew term 'adam' means 'humanity'; this also being the case in Gen. 5:2. It is only from chapter 2 that Adam is used as a proper noun for the male: but see comments by Trible later in this chapter.

The creation of the woman is framed by two perspectives: the superiority of the man over the animals ('no suitable helper was found' — 2:20) and the relatedness of the woman to the man ('now bone of my bone and flesh of my flesh' — 2:23). The creation of the woman meant the creation of someone just like the man. This is borne out by the way woman's creation is portrayed: she is not a separate creation from the dust of the earth but is made from the man — if she was from the dust as separate creation we would need to debate where she fitted in the divine order. The woman being created of the 'same stuff' also lessens the weight that can be given to the argument that she was created after the man and therefore inferior.

Indeed, even on the issue of subsequent creation, Phyllis Trible makes some astute observations which should challenge the normally accepted 'fact' of the male created first and the female subsequent. She considers that the first human creature is 'neither male or female nor a combination of both'.[5] On the basis of the pun on the Hebrew words *adam* (man) and *adama* (earth) she calls this original creature 'earth-creature'. Once the woman is created from the body of the earth-creature, it is only from that point on that we have male and female human beings. Thus both males and females are created simultaneously from the original earth-creature. This model has much to commend it, and if adopted would remove any discussions regarding the significance of the prior creation of the male. Although I am attracted to her model, I will continue to operate with the more classic definition that the male was created first as this has been used to endorse male supremacy, and we will also have to face this issue when we come to the text in 1 Timothy 2:13 that 'Adam was formed first.'[6]

---

[5]*God and the Rhetoric of Sexuality* (Overtures to Biblical Theology 2, Philadelphia: Fortress, 1978), p. 98.

[6]There is a very key point that needs to be made here, namely the requirement to distinguish between the usage of the OT within a NT context, and the meaning of the original OT text. For example, Paul's interpretation of the Hagar story (Gal.

It is the description of Eve as 'a helper suitable for' Adam that has caused some to suggest that this term indicates the creation of woman in an inferior position. However the word helper (Hebrew: *ezer*) does not normally carry with it the concept of inferiority. Indeed the immediate context itself indicates that the animals were inferior and incapable of being this 'helper' to Adam. This does not necessarily indicate that the woman is created equal, but the narrative is suggesting that whereas there is a contrast between the animals and Adam, there is comparison to be understood between Adam and Eve. Beyond the immediate context, we discover that the term is used of God some fifteen times in the Old Testament (out of a total of nineteen occurrences) and is certainly not used in those contexts of inferiority![7] The term 'helper' in this chapter is further qualified by the phrase 'suitable for him' (Hebrew: *kenegdo*). This Hebrew word consists of three components[8] and would come out in a literal translation as 'as opposite / in front of / over against him', and therefore perhaps should be translated with the sense of 'corresponding to him'. Raymond Ortlund Jr. says on the basis of this phrase that, 'The woman is a helper suitable for the man, on his level, in contrast to the animals', and the

---

4:21-31) does not determine the historical meaning of the passage (Gen. 16); nor does his interpretation of the Exodus story of crossing the Red Sea determine the meaning of the story in the original context. OT stories can be used in creative ways, and there is a very real sense in which NT writers can advance ad hoc arguments to help support their case. Thus *even if* Paul were to quote the OT creation narratives to support the idea of the priority of men over women, this would not in itself determine the original meaning.

[7]See Mary Evans, *Woman in the Bible* (Exeter: Paternoster, 1983), p. 16. I note that the use of the word 'helper' should not, by itself, be used as an indicator of inferiority (or indeed superiority). Unless the immediate context demanded an understanding that the woman was created inferior we should not infer this from the word.

[8]The preposition *neged* with meanings such as: 'in front of, opposite, over against'; a prefix *k* meaning 'like' or 'as'; and a suffix *o* meaning 'him'.

woman is 'his counterpart and equal'.[9] The conclusion of this part of the narrative is that we are being introduced to the concept of the man and woman together fulfilling the God-given commission: they are to be partners together, so much so that in marriage they are to be 'one flesh' (Genesis 2:24).

This last verse quoted raises two interesting points. We read that the man leaves the home of his parents to be joined to his wife. Does this indicate that the first marriages were matrilocal? Secondly, in leaving his parents he is to join (Hebrew: *dabaq*) himself to his wife. This word is often used of the inferior party joining themselves to someone stronger for protection. So for example, Ruth joins herself, as a foreigner without any rights, to Naomi the Jewess who has rights in the land of Israel (Ruth 1:14). In a similar vein Israel is instructed to join herself to God (Deuteronomy 10:20; 11:22 ; Joshua 23:8; etc.).[10] To suggest, on the basis of this verse, that the man is inferior to the wife, would be reading considerably too much into the verse; but conversely to read inferiority into the term 'helper' would be to do likewise in the other direction.

Before making a comment on 'creation-order' there is one other aspect that needs to be addressed briefly. It is suggested that Adam's naming of the woman indicates his superiority over her (Genesis 2:23). Evans points out that we do not encounter in this verse the normal naming formula. This 'formula' contains the verb 'to call' and the noun 'name' — which does occur when Adam names the animals in verse 19. In verse 23, however, these terms do not occur together and the term

---

[9]'Male-Female Equality and Male Headship', chapter 3 of Piper & Grudem (eds.), *Recovering Biblical Manhood and Womanhood*, 103f. Ortlund does not propose women having an equal role and position to men, so his acknowledgement indicates the all-but-universal acceptance that *kenegdo* indicates an equality between the genders. Trible, op. cit., suggests that the helper is 'the companion who is neither subordinate or superior; one who alleviates isolation through identity' (p. 90).

[10]Evans, *Woman*, p. 17.

'woman' is not a name but simply a common noun indicating gender.[11] It is therefore highly doubtful, in this context, how much can be drawn from this 'naming' episode.

As far as creation order is concerned, I think we need to exercise a great deal of care that we do not read into the text what we have been taught rather than read the text at face value. Sometimes it is suggested that the priority of the man over the woman is reflected in the fact that the man was created before the woman, and that she found her purpose in relation to him (as helper). The latter point has been looked at above and I have suggested that the term 'helper' in this context cannot be shown to indicate an inferior position for the woman in relation to the man. The former point would be a very difficult position to insist upon. Calvin notes the tenuousness of the argument of the superiority of the man over the woman based on the chronological sequence. Making a comment on Paul's words in 1 Timothy 2 Calvin states that, 'Paul's argument that woman is subject because she was created second does not seem very strong, for John the Baptist went before Christ in time and yet was far inferior to him.'[12] Let me further illustrate by giving another reading of Scripture that could actually be used to endorse an opposite position to the one that claims superiority for the man.

---

[11]Evans, ibid., p. 16. However, it is possible to read Gen. 3:20 (a naming that seemingly comes after the 'naming' incident of Gen. 2:23) as containing the naming formula and might indicate Adam taking authority over his wife — even if so this is in a post-fall scenario. The context, though, suggests that we have here a creative 'prophetic' word over Eve.

[12]From his commentary on 1 Timothy, quoted in Kevin Giles, 'A Critique of the 'Novel' Contemporary Interpretation of 1 Timothy 2:9-15 Given in the book, Women in the Church.' Part II, *Evangelical Quarterly*, Vol. LXXII, No. 3 (July, 2000), pp. 195f.

If we are to make an assumption that creation becomes more complex as it develops, so Adam is superior to the animals.[13] But as the woman is created after the man, as the pinnacle of all creation she clearly is the superior one. Perhaps this could further be endorsed by grasping the fact that the serpent came first to Eve because she was appointed as 'boss' of the earth. He knew that if he could deceive her then everything she ruled over would automatically be his, which of course would include Adam! Could this be the underlying reasons why the patriarch Abraham was told to do whatever his wife told him to do (Genesis 21:12), and why Jesus appeared first to women after the resurrection?

I do not endorse the (tongue-in-cheek) creation-order account as outlined above, but merely use it to point out that it is all too easy to misread Scripture according to our presuppositions. If we look to this chapter of Genesis to discover a revealed order, we surely need to agree with Jewett when he says: 'So far as Genesis 2 is concerned, sexual hierarchy must be read into the text, it is not required by the text.'[14]

In conclusion both accounts of creation indicate that men and women are created equally in the image of God and are called to exercise their God-given authority together in partnership. One other point that is worth making is that even *if* we were to have found a strict hierarchical order in these chapters of Genesis, we would not have been able to accept this as the final word. Through his resurrection Christ has

---

[13]I am aware that the order of creation in the second account is somewhat different to the one I have outlined above (based on Gen. 1). In the second account it appears as if the man (or earth creature, as per Trible) is created before the animals. But my point remains for it is simply that to insist on being created prior to another creature does not in and of itself prove superiority. The whole point of the Gen. 2 narrative seems to centre around mutuality rather than who is created first. Only in woman is a suitable helper found.

[14]Paul Jewett, *Man as Male and Female* (Grand Rapids: Eerdmans, 1975), p. 126.

inaugurated a whole new creation, which does not simply restore the old creation but transcends it.[15]

1.2 Genesis 3: Human Fall

If the first two chapters indicate how things began, chapter 3 is a sad record of how things went wrong. Chapter 3 will not indicate how things should be, but give us the state of affairs that result from sin. Once sin arrived disruption was brought to the whole world and particularly to the area of relationships. It is no surprise to find that from this point onwards tension is present in all relationships, including marriage.

In due course we will focus on Genesis 3:16 and its statement on male/female relationships, but prior to this there are a number of points we need to consider:

1. There is no indication that woman is condemned for making a decision independent of the man. She is not judged for taking the masculine role but is in the wrong because she enters into disobedience. To argue that she took the 'masculine role' is to read into the text what is not explicitly there.[16]

2. Adam is not judged *simply* because he listened to his wife (Genesis 3:17) in the sense that a husband who listens to his wife is sinning. It was the substitution of her voice for God's that was the problem. Had Eve endorsed God's command and Adam had failed to heed her voice, we would be reading 'because you did not listen to the voice of your wife'.

---

[15]This is a key point that is often missed. For instance, in the substantial work edited by Piper and Grudem, *Recovering Biblical Manhood and Womanhood*, there is no discussion of Christ as 'Last Adam'. So on p. 109 we read that 'Christian redemption does not redefine creation; it restores creation, so that wives learn godly submission and husbands learn godly headship.'

[16]As per David Pawson, *Leadership is Male* (Crowborough: Highland Books, 1988), p. 23; and Ortlund in Grudem & Piper (eds), *Manhood*, p. 107f.

In other words we must be careful to keep to the facts, which are that the man and woman are judged for disobeying the commands of God.[17]

3. To argue that Adam was the first to sin theologically[18] because he allowed the woman to lead (i.e. a reversal of roles) is not the result of a clear exegesis of the passage, but the result of an unwarranted reading of a presupposition into the text. There is another way of looking at the text which is that Genesis 3:6 suggests that Adam was present while the dialogue between the serpent and Eve was taking place. It is possible that he is the first to sin because he simply stood by without speaking up — i.e., he was culpable because he was passive. This would have been equally true of the woman had she stood there observing the situation and allowed the man to eat of the forbidden fruit without speaking up for the truth. (James 4:17 — 'Anyone, then, who knows the right thing to do and fails to do it, commits sin' (NRSV).)

4. If we embrace this basic argument that the fundamental problem in the Fall was role reversal, we would need to ask a basic question: what was the feminine role before the Fall? We know that Adam and Eve were to live in partnership — in their togetherness they were created in the image of God and they were both commissioned with regard to the earth. One can only assume that they flowed in harmony together before the entrance of sin and that the question of leadership was, at most, purely academic.[19]

5. The crux of the matter is that once we suggest that Adam's mistake was to put himself in the feminine role (by following his wife) the issue becomes clouded. The problem was that he followed her in disobedience. And it would be equally true that, if the woman had

---

[17]See Ortlund in Grudem & Piper (eds), ibid., p. 110 for an example of going beyond the text. This is somewhat adjusted in his note 50.

[18]Pawson, *Leadership*, p. 23.

[19]There might well have been distinct roles prior to the fall, but those are not specified. The point being made above is that the roles are certainly not laid out in any clear hierarchical fashion.

followed the man into sin, we would still be in the mess we are in! We need only to look at the case of Ananias and Sapphira to see this (Acts 5:1-11). She is equally judged alongside her husband — she could not plead in her defence that she was simply fulfilling the feminine role!

6. Eve did not use deception as an excuse: rather, she explained the reality. Adam, however, blamed Eve, and ultimately blamed God for the problem, refusing to take responsibility for the situation. So to argue he is more fit to lead than Eve (as some would from Paul's statements regarding Eve's deception in 1 Timothy 2:11-15) is rather strange.[20] If subsequent to the Fall God ordains the man to lead we might be forced, on the basis of the evidence of Adam's irresponsibility, to suggest that this was a curse and not a blessing. If so we would expect this curse to be reversed through the death of Christ.

7. They are both punished — God treats both as responsible beings. The wife is not judged as a servant of the husband but as an individual in her own right.[21]

---

[20]See Pawson, *Leadership*, p. 23.

[21]The fact that God speaks to Adam first (Gen. 3:9ff.) might be seen as the strongest point in favour of the view that there was some hierarchy of relationship already in existence. This approach of God to Adam certainly *could* be understood to indicate that Adam was the one in overall responsibility. I would counter with two perspectives: the first asking the question of the narrative itself. Is the narrative really seeking to make that point? Secondly, and perhaps in some way related to the first, I accept that the Scriptures are written from a patriarchal perspective and therefore there is a male bias within them. By this I do not mean that we should feel free to 'exorcise' patriarchal texts, but that we must give weight to the culture in which they were written. They are written from the masculine perspective. This is not to detract from their divine inspiration, but simply to acknowledge that there are also human elements within Scripture. The first point relates to an exegetical issue (what is the text saying, and on this there will always be some divergence) while the second one relates more to hermeneutical matters (what do they mean and how do we apply them, and on this there will be a greater divergence).

8. The result of sin was a break in the relationship between God and humanity — and also to the relationship between husband and wife. It is to this husband/wife tension that I now want to turn.

1.2.1 The gender-war (Genesis 3:16)

In this passage we read 'Your desire will be for your husband, and he will rule over you' which is God's statement as to how the relationship will now be outworked. It is not a statement of the 'perfect will' of God and needs to be seen in the same light as the other consequences of the Fall, such as the ground being cursed. We do not accuse those who seek to control the 'thorns and thistles' as defying God's order! Biblically, such people are recognising that this is not how things should be and are seeking to counteract the *un*natural order of things.[22]

There is general acceptance that this verse has a parallel in the next chapter of Genesis which records God's word to Cain. Cain is informed that, 'sin is crouching at the door; it desires to have you, but you must master it' (Genesis 4:7). Both these verses have the words 'desire' (Hebrew: *tesuqah*) and 'rule/master' (Hebrew: *mashal*), and in as much as there is an all but exact parallel of language, I suggest that the latter verse can help us understand the former.

In the Cain situation we have sin personified and a resultant clash of 'wills'. There is a battle in which Cain must exert his will for future approval. In the Adam / Eve situation there is also a battle, with the battle over who will be dominant. We are here introduced to the gender-war with the explanation that the man will win the conflict. (We should note, unlike the Cain situation, we do not have the statement that 'your husband *must* rule over you'; it simply says he *will* rule over you.)

---

[22]Although it is true that it is the serpent and the ground that are cursed and not the people, the narrative is presented in such a way that the effects on the serpent, the ground and the people all result from the original human sin. The effects then render an adverse change to all three 'parties', and whether we term those a curse or not, the effects are unnatural.

There are other interpretations given to Genesis 3:16. It is suggested by those who see very distinctive male/female roles in the creation narratives that this verse endorses that original male headship, stating that the man is to rule over the woman. However to argue this is to remove the verse from its immediate context which deals with the *consequences* of sin for humanity's relationships. The verse is a statement of fact without any sense of divine approval for the relational tension.[23]

A very different interpretation is given by Phyllis Trible. She understands this verse to indicate that the woman desires the original unity between the male and female but that the man will not reciprocate. In wishing to rule over her he corrupts both himself and his wife. Trible says that:

> His supremacy is neither a divine right nor a male prerogative. Her subordination is neither a divine decree nor the female destiny. Both their positions result from shared disobedience. God describes this consequence but does not prescribe it as punishment.'[24]

I agree wholeheartedly with the quote from Trible but understand, in the light of the parallel words addressed to Cain, the desire of the woman to be less pure than she indicates. The result of the Fall is a tension: the woman will desire to rule her husband, but, in the end, the husband will tend to dominate the woman.

By extension, history bears testimony that women have been ruled over by men in most societies, and even within the record of history that is recorded in Scripture this tends to be the case. In our first chapter we saw that authority flows from mutual submission and that corrupted authority tends toward authoritarianism and demands

---

[23]Contra Ortlund in Piper & Grudem, op. cit., p. 109.
[24]*Rhetoric*, p. 128.

subjection from the other party. The picture we are introduced to in Genesis 3:16 is simply that of corrupted authority.

1.3 Post-Eden Scriptures

These early chapters of Genesis have been important as they establish how it was at the beginning (partnership to fulfil the commission), and how sin impacted this relationship (division and strife). It is not surprising therefore that in the remainder of the Old Testament we generally see women with inferior roles to men within society.

It should be understood that Old Testament law does not reveal the will of God — that privilege is reserved for the revelation that takes place in Jesus. We do expect the law to point society in the right direction, but the 'destination' is Jesus. For example, the law said 'do not murder', but Jesus intensified this stating that sinful anger was unacceptable. Through the law we would expect that the woman's place within Israel might well be protected, and thereby improved, when compared to society around, but that her role would still fall short of the will of God. It is for this reason that we will simply note that the Old Testament picture is of women tending to have an inferior role within both the religious and social spheres. Her normal place was the home but the notable exceptions to this norm are what I want to highlight. These examples give some insight into the possibilities for women when God comes and anoints them.

1.3.1 Miriam, Deborah and Huldah

Miriam is said to lead Israel alongside Moses and Aaron. Micah 6:4 says, 'I sent Moses to lead you, also Aaron and Miriam.' The Hebrew here has the literal meaning of 'before' which the NIV (I believe) rightly interprets as leadership. Each of these three had specific leadership roles: Moses as lawgiver, Aaron as priest, and Miriam as prophetess (Exodus 15:20). The significance of her role is further borne out by her joint challenge with Aaron to Moses' role (Numbers 12) and her subsequent judgement.

Deborah was a woman who exercised leadership in the political, military, civil and religious spheres of Israel's life (Judges 4). If the other Judges were leaders (and they most certainly were)[25] there is no reason to suggest that she was not a significant leader within Israel at that time.

Huldah exercised a prophetic ministry and the king sent five national male leaders to her for advice as to the instructions of the Lord concerning the book of the law which Josiah had found (2 Chronicles 34:14-28). Given that she was a contemporary of Jeremiah and Zephaniah it is not possible to resort to the (appalling) argument that God uses a woman when he cannot find a man.

1.3.2 Proverbs 31: the ideal woman

The ideal woman does not sit at home doing the washing up and darning her husband's socks. Far from it she is a (or perhaps even *the*) major contributor to the welfare and upkeep of her family. Perhaps she is closer to the original 'career woman' than many would like to believe.

Most English versions describe her as a 'noble' woman. The Hebrew text has the word *chayil* which carries the sense of 'strong, efficient, forceful'. This comes across in the 'Bible' of the early church, the Greek translation known as the Septuagint (normally abbreviated to LXX) which states that the ideal woman is a 'manly' or 'masculine' one!

1.3.3 Women leaders as a judgement?

Isaiah 3:12 has been used to communicate that women in leadership should be seen as a curse. It reads, 'Youths oppress my people, women rule over them. O my people, your guides lead you astray; they turn you from the path'. The verse clearly fits in the context of judgement (see verses 1-4).

---

[25]The verb 'to judge' is used some 20 times in the book of Judges and is also used of Samuel and the kings (1 Sam. 8:5-6).

There is some debate as to the meaning of the Hebrew text. It can be translated as the NIV (above) or as with the LXX: 'As for my people, tax-gatherers glean them and exactors rule over them.' This valid translation also fits the context, for as we read further we see that God takes issue with elders and princes (NB: masculine) who have oppressed the people. We also read later in the same chapter (verses 16-17) of a judgement against the rich women who were more interested in fashion and status than in justice. So if it is a reference to women, it needs to be seen in that setting. I conclude that if the reference is to women it is not to women in general but to these rich exploitative women.

1.4   Women in the first-century Jewish world

We have looked at the place of women within the life of Israel and accept that they had an inferior role to men, seldom rising to levels of leadership. We are now fast approaching the point in Israel's history where Jesus arrives on the stage and it is time to paint the scene that Jesus encounters.

The Judaism of Jesus' day had a strongly negative attitude towards women. A woman's sphere was within the family, and the father or husband had extraordinary powers over her. The laws of inheritance, betrothal and divorce were all heavily weighted in the male's favour. Within this negative setting, there were exceptions where women were taught the Torah[26] and there is even evidence that Rabbi Meir's wife, Beruriah, was consulted on specific points related to the oral law.[27] Those, however, were the exception.

---

[26]This was only ever the case where the rabbi who taught the woman was either a husband or master to the woman in question. Jesus broke totally with tradition in his relationships with women. See Ben Witherington III, *Women and the Genesis of Christianity* (Cambridge: Cambridge University Press, 1990), p. 111.
[27]Witherington, ibid., p. 7.

The examples below are more generally representative of a woman's place within the Judaism of Jesus' day. Rabbis generally refused to teach women — advising, in the strongest possible terms, that to teach women the Torah was tantamount to lechery; the Jewish historian, Josephus, stated that women were inferior to men in every way; there is a Jewish prayer which says, 'Praise be to God he has not created me a Gentile; praise be to God he has not created me a woman; praise be to God he has not created me an ignorant man';[28] there are no known examples of women reading the Torah in the synagogue in Jesus' day; the women were separated in both Temple and synagogue; and women could not make up the quorum necessary to found a synagogue.[29]

Although Judaism has never been monolithic, and the attitude toward women would have varied from rabbi to rabbi, it is clear that women were treated as second-class within the Jewish culture of Jesus' time. Evans concludes with the words, 'As far as first century Judaism is concerned there is no doubt at all that the place of woman was not equal to that of the man. Women were subordinate and inferior to men in religion, in society in general and also in the home and family.'[30] In comparison to the Old Testament she suggests that 'it is possible to see a dramatic decline in the position and status of women in every sphere'.[31] Jesus' attitudes, teaching and behaviour need to be seen against that background — and I suggest once they are, he will be seen to be very radical indeed.

2.   Jesus and women

The life of Jesus and the relational dynamic that he modelled was a challenge to the established order — and ever remains so. His response

---

[28]Babylonian Talmud Menahoth 43b.
[29]Witherington, *Women*, p. 246.
[30]Evans, *Woman*, p. 36.
[31]Ibid., p. 37.

to women and all marginalised groups reveal a God who lifts up the humble and resists the proud. Among the common people who heard him gladly were women who found a new sense of identity in their encounter with him. Jesus was truly counterculture in his attitude towards, and interaction with, women. I will highlight some of these counter-cultural aspects below.

2.1 Jesus fulfilling 'women's' roles

Jesus fulfilled roles that were traditionally fulfilled by women. He cooked a meal, washed feet[32] and allowed children to sit on his knee. He redefined what it meant to be a man and therefore also what it meant to be a woman.

He also used feminine imagery to describe his prophetic role when he likens it to a mother hen seeking to care for her chicks (Matt. 23:37-39). Witherington states that 'it should not be overlooked that Jesus takes on a role normally performed by a Jewish woman of publicly and "prophetically" mourning over Jerusalem'.[33]

2.2 Men and lust

In Palestinian Judaism the woman was always blamed for a man's lust. If a woman was seen in public with an exposed face she could expect that men would lust after her.[34] Jesus, however, did not blame the woman but firmly placed the responsibility with the man for his behaviour (Matthew 5:27-30). In Jesus' new order, men and women were to look at each other differently: women were no longer to be seen as sex-

---

[32]The washing of feet was so menial that a Hebrew slave could not be enforced to do so. A Gentile slave might be required to fulfil this role, but it was expected that a wife would wash her husband's feet and children the feet of their father. See: Walter Wink, *Engaging the Powers* (Minneapolis: Fortress, 1992), p. 112; Leon Morris, *John*, New International Commentary (Grand Rapids: Eerdmans, 1971), p. 617, n. 23.

[33]Witherington, *Women*, p. 61.

[34]Keener, *...And Marries Another* (Peabody, MA: Hendrikson, 1991), p. 18.

objects but as people of equal value.[35] Jesus radicalised the meaning of lust and adultery to include even the mental act of dehumanising women. He did so, not to shower guilt on men, but to counter the self-righteousness of those men who were technically free of adultery under the law, but continued to treat women as objects.

2.3   Jesus: conversations and contact with women

Respectable women were not to speak to men in public,[36] yet Jesus conversed freely with them (John 4:4-42; Mark 5:33-34//Luke 8:47-48; Mark 7:24-30//Matthew 15:21-28). Indeed two of the longest conversations recorded in the Gospels were with women. In one of those conversations (with the Samaritan woman) he uniquely reveals himself as the Messiah, and John records the disciples' horror upon their return when they saw that he was 'talking with a woman' (John 4:27).

A woman was not to touch any man other than her husband,[37] but Jesus was touched by women and also touched them. He even allowed a woman (and probably a prostitute at that) to wipe away the tears with her uncovered hair (Luke 7:36-50).[38]

---

[35]In Mark's recording of Jesus' teaching on divorce he also gave them equal rights for divorce as men: something unknown in the Jewish world (Mk. 10:12).

[36]Witherington, *Women*, p. 73.

[37]Walter Wink, *Engaging the Powers*, p. 129.

[38]Only a prostitute would have her hair loosed in public. Keener, *Paul, Women and Wives* (Peabody, MA: Hendrikson, 1992), gives extensive evidence that a woman's hair was seen as the point of focus of a man's lust. A quote from Keener will indicate the reason for Simon's horror in this story, 'A woman uncovering her head could be described as nearing the final stages in seducing a man. Jewish teachers permitted loosing a woman's hair only in the case of an adulterous woman, who was publicly shamed by exposure to the sight of men; but even in this case they warned that it should not be done with women whose hair was extremely beautiful, lest the young priests be moved to lust' (p. 29).

2.4   Women as disciples

2.4.1 Daughter of Abraham

He calls the woman bent over with a spinal disorder for eighteen years a 'daughter of Abraham' (Luke 13:10-17). This term applied to an individual is unknown in Judaism and by using the term Jesus is declaring that she is a full member of the covenant community in her own right. He not only heals her but restores her true dignity.[39] In the story Jesus defends the right of the woman and confronts the male leadership in no uncertain terms calling them 'hypocrites'!

2.4.2 Women's roles: to do the will of God

In Luke 11:27 we read that a woman cried out, 'Blessed is the mother who gave you birth and nursed you' which reflects something of the current view of the day. A woman gained status through marriage, in marriage her role was to bear children, and if she could bear a male child then she would be truly blessed. Further, if that male child was a rabbi of the stature of Jesus she would be considered greatly blessed. This is the world-view of this particular woman and it spontaneously comes from her lips. Jesus however, gives a reply which challenges her world-view and gave women the same role as men: 'Blessed rather are those who hear the word of God and obey it' (Luke 11:28). Women and men are equally called to be disciples.

2.4.3 Mary the disciple

Mary is described as sitting at the feet of Jesus (Luke 10:39), a technical term of one who made themselves a disciple of the teacher (cf. Paul who sat at the feet of Gamaliel in Acts 22:3). Jesus even informed Martha (who was complying with the culture of the day in giving hospitality) that Mary had chosen the 'better' role.

---

[39]Witherington, *Women*, p.79.

2.4.4 Followers to the end

Women were among those who followed him, and some of the wealthier women supported him financially (Luke 8:1-3). A number of these women came from Galilee and even followed Jesus as far as Jerusalem for they are present at the time of his death (see Mark 15:40-41). This (as also for the male disciples) must have had implications for their responsibilities back in Galilee. These women were literal followers of Jesus — something no other Jewish rabbi would ever allow.[40]

2.4.5 Women witnesses and the Easter Event

It is women who became the primary witnesses of the final events of Jesus' earthly career and of the resurrection. Other than the beloved disciple (John 19:26-27) it appears that the only disciples who stood by Jesus were the women.[41] They are the witnesses of both his death and resurrection. This has great significance for Josephus tells us that a woman's testimony was not to be trusted,[42] yet Jesus allows the women to be those who will witness these events, and it is Mary that he instructs to tell the men to go to Galilee and meet with him (Matthew 28:7,10; Mark 16:7; John 20:13-18). So in making the women the primary witnesses, Jesus is redeeming the traditional view of the untrustworthiness of women. The women had gone to the tomb to

---

[40]Wink, op. cit., not only notes the uniqueness of Jesus in having women followers when he states that, 'it was without known precedent for women to travel as disciples with a teacher', but that for women such as Joanna it would have meant that she probably had to leave home, family, and husband in order to follow Jesus (p. 131).

[41]Luke 23:49 speaks of all those who knew him and the women who followed him being present (albeit at a distance) at the cross. If there are men who are among those present, Luke clearly singles out the women as the significant witnesses for the verbs used here are feminine participles (followed and watched). Normally even one man among a crowd of women would demand that the participles used were masculine — so either no men are included, or Luke, in the strongest possible way, wants to focus on the women.

[42]Josephus, *The Antiquities of the Jews*, Book IV, viii.15.

perform a traditional role (to anoint the corpse) but they leave commissioned with a most untraditional role (reliable witnesses and proclaimers of the resurrection). He views them as trustworthy; they are the ones he chooses to be the primary witnesses of the central event of the Christian faith. Witherington concludes, 'Thus, the women are treated not as emissaries to the disciples but as true disciples who are worthy of receiving special revelation about Jesus'.[43]

2.4.6 Women used as examples

Luke's gospel in particular is full of examples relating to women from the life of Jesus. This is probably due to the fact that he sees Jesus' central message being one of liberation to the oppressed (Luke 4:16-30). For Luke, women are among the oppressed that Jesus came to liberate.[44] One example of the elevation of the oppressed is shown in Luke's record that it is a woman who models true giving (Luke 21:1-4).

Luke, more than any other gospel writer, structures his writing in such a way that there is a clear male-female parallel. He often presents Jesus as healing a man and then a woman, or telling a parable about a woman and following it with a parable concerning a man. By so doing he is placing men and women on the same footing.

At times he even goes beyond placing them on equal footing and weights his narrative toward women. The Queen of Sheba, for example, is praised at the expense of certain male Jewish leaders (Luke 11:31; see also 7:36-50 and 13:10-17 for this emphasis of women over men).

---

[43]Witherington, *Women*, pp. 202f.
[44]Gustavo Gutiérrez, *A Theology of Liberation* (London: SCM, 1988) has caught something of this feel by his use of the term 'absent'. He states that 'our time bears the imprint of the new presence of those who used to be "absent" from our society and from our church. By "absent" I mean: of little or no importance, and without the opportunity to give expression themselves to their sufferings, their comraderies, their plans, their hopes' (p. xx). He describes the women of Latin America as the doubly oppressed and marginalised. Such a description would have been highly accurate for the women of Jesus' time.

In the birth narratives it is Elizabeth and Mary, not Zechariah and Joseph who are the first to receive the message of Christ's coming. Anna and Simeon take part in the Temple scene but it can be argued that Anna has the more prominent role. Simeon is ready now to die, but Anna takes her revelation and declares it to others. It is possible that Luke intends us to see Simeon as representative of the old prophetic order which is ready to die and Anna as a representative of the new order — the order of equality when the Spirit of prophecy is outpoured on all flesh (male and female) resulting in public proclamation and witness (Acts 2 and Pentecost).

Also in Luke's gospel we find Jesus freely using a story about a woman to illustrate the love of God (Luke 15:8-10). In effect he is saying, 'God is like a woman who searches for her lost coin.' To use such blatantly feminine imagery must have been very offensive in the patriarchal society of Jesus' day.

2.5 Concluding remarks

In Jesus, the great reversal had taken place: the first would be last and the last would be first. He put men and women on equal terms before God and broke the power of the abusive patriarchy of his day. His followers were not to call anyone 'father' (Matthew 23:9): those who do the will of God are his 'brother, sister or mother' (Mark 3:31-35; NB no mention of father), and those who left all for his sake will receive back houses, brothers, sisters, mothers, children and land — but no fathers (Mark 10:29-30).[45] Jesus is redefining family relationships for his followers and he is redeeming the title 'father' by only allowing it to be applied to God.[46] God is not to be seen as one made in the image of an

---

[45] I owe these observations to Wink, *Engaging the Powers*, particularly chapter 6, pp. 109-137.

[46] I am not suggesting that he literally forbade anyone to call their biological male parent 'father', nor that someone could not be referred to as one's spiritual father, otherwise why would Paul use the term of his own relationship with the Corinthian believers. What is implied is that any mode of relating that continued

earthly father, rather earthly fathers must now model themselves on the heavenly Father.

Those who had previously been 'absent' were now made present in and through the ministry of Jesus.

There are two key issues that need to be addressed in the life of Jesus. The first is that of the twelve apostles who were all male, and the second is the fact that Jesus himself was male. The first issue we will address at this point, the latter will be picked up in chapter 8 of this book.

Excursus: A note on the choice of twelve male apostles

Assuming (rightly) that there is great significance in the choosing of the apostles there are two possibilities as to the reason for this choice. The first possibility would be in giving a pointer to the future while the second would draw its significance from the past. If the choice was pointing forward then it could indicate that male leadership should be the norm within the Christian community. This is unlikely, for then we would probably also need to suggest that Jews should have precedence over Gentiles as far as leadership is concerned (those first apostles being Jewish as well as male). A much more likely reason is that Jesus deliberately chose twelve 'sons' to show the clear link with the past. In order to demonstrate prophetically that he is forming a new Israel, or more accurately, forming Israel anew, he, in the same way that Israel was originally founded on the twelve sons of Jacob (Luke 22:30; Matthew 21:43), founds his work and people on the choice of twelve male apostles (sons). If this is so the choosing of the twelve apostles would not then have any bearing on the gender of leadership within the (future) Christian community.

---

to give males an advantage was to come to an end. Although one could not insist that Jesus overthrew all concept of patriarchy, it is clear that he broke the power of every abusive form.

This viewpoint seems to borne out by the choosing of Matthias after the death of Judas Iscariot to make up their number (Acts 1:15-26). Spencer comments that 'the significance of such an action is obvious. The number twelve represents the whole nation of Israel under the ancestral headship of the twelve sons of Jacob/Israel.'[47] This band of disciples saw themselves in direct continuity with Israel, as the faithful remnant through whom God was now going to fulfil his purposes. The twelve foundations of this remnant were to be kept intact for the promise of restoration was beginning with them.[48] Fellow Jews could remain as part of God's people only as they responded to the Jewish Messiah and joined this band — hence Peter's appeal to the people is to repent otherwise they 'will be completely cut off from among his people' (Acts 3:23, this can only be understood as God's people; the apostles seeing themselves as the restored Israel). Jesus indicated something similar with his words to Israel. He said that they were in danger of having the kingdom taken from them and given to another nation (Matthew 21:43). This would have been very provocative for, like Jacob before him, he is standing with twelve sons and a wider company of mixed gender people. Jesus informs them that though they are Jacob's physical descendants, they are in danger of losing the kingdom and by implication it is Jesus' band of followers that are being promised it.[49]

So the choosing of the twelve as male is to continue the link with the past. This new movement is not new in the sense of 'now for

---

[47]F. Scott Spencer, *Acts* (Readings: A New Biblical Commentary; Sheffield: Sheffield Academic Press, 1997), p. 29.

[48]Max Turner, *Power From on High* (Sheffield: Sheffield Academic Press, 1996), shows that the outpouring of the Spirit was to mark and effect the restoration of Israel. Hence the response of Jesus in Acts 1:8 is a response to the disciples' question of Acts 1:6. The restoration, and redefinition, of Israel is a major theme within Acts. (See also the Isaianic passages such as Is. 32:15; 43:10; 49:6.)

[49]See also Luke 12:32 where Jesus uses the description of the people of God as the flock gathered together to fulfil his purpose. Zech. 9:16 applies this imagery to eschatological Israel, restored by God. Jesus applies this to the disciples indicating that the restoration is beginning in him and those who follow him.

something completely different'; rather it is new in the sense of God's redemptive activity entering a new phase. In the light of the above, I do not consider that the maleness of the apostolic band has any significance on the leadership issue.

End of Excursus

Having looked at the life and practices of Jesus we can now look at Paul and we will return to the Pauline texts that seem to restrict women in chapter 6.

3.   Paul and women

3.1   Acts: women in the Pauline world

We have seen that the gospel writers record the liberation that Jesus brought to all who were oppressed. Acts likewise records the outworking of this liberation. The Spirit is poured out on all flesh, and of particular note is the element of liberation involved in this outpouring. Age, gender and social class are no barrier for this outpouring is for 'all flesh'. As far as women are concerned they are specifically mentioned by Peter / Luke twice: 'your sons and your daughters shall prophesy', and the Spirit will be poured out on 'my slaves, both men and women' (Acts 2:17,18). Luke notes the presence of women within the community for he states that both men and women came to believe (Acts 5:14, and Acts 17:4,12, where he writes that a number of prominent women were converted). Beyond this we can note that Saul leaves for Damascus to imprison not only men but also women (Acts 9:2);[50] Philip had four daughters who prophesied (Acts 21:9); and both Ananias and Sapphira are equally judged (Acts 5:1-11).

There are two women who probably had regular meetings in their homes. In Joppa there is a specific reference to Tabitha (also

---

[50]Spencer, *Acts*, p. 83, suggests that the arrest of women and men gives 'a hint of women's influence in the developing church: they are important enough to be arrested and imprisoned!'

known as Dorcas) as a disciple in Acts 9:36. This is of particular significance as it is the only use in the New Testament of a feminine form for disciple (Greek: *mathetria*). Spencer maintains that she was almost certainly the community host, and although this would not have guaranteed 'her position as community *head*,' Spencer says that 'within a patronage society it certainly points in that direction.'[51] Even if Spencer has rather overstated his case, it is useful to be challenged to think again as to this possibility — and also to realise that we often reflect back into Acts our own views of church leadership (were they really as defined as we have made them in our churches?). The second reference is to Mary, the mother of John Mark. She is a wealthy lady who acted as the female host to the prayer meeting in Acts 12:12-17. She could well have been the regular female host of a local house church. 'Whether she also functions as a leader and teacher in this community, as we might assume, is left open in the narrative.'[52]

Paul, however, has sometimes been accused of misogyny, mainly on the basis of some interpretations of certain Pauline passages, but I believe there is a very clear overall egalitarian approach in Paul with respect to women. We will first examine Paul's interaction with women in Acts and then the references to women in his letters.

3.2   Paul: women in Acts

Paul begins a church in Philippi with women. He goes to the place of prayer by the river and Lydia responds to the gospel message (Acts 16:13-15). Although a Jewish synagogue could not be formed on the basis of women, Paul is prepared to found a church on them. Women

---

[51]Ibid., p. 108. Spencer might be going too far in his assumptions, but points out that she was recognised as a benefactress, and with no mention of a husband we are given a picture of Tabitha as a single woman of independent means, likely the owner of the house. He posits that she 'regularly hosted the Joppa assembly for occasions of worship and fellowship — other than her own funeral!'

[52]Ibid., p. 127. Her wealth is indicated by two factors in the narrative. Her house has a significant gate and she has a maid-servant in her employ.

might have been periphery to the Jewish faith but not the Christian faith. Witherington comments that Lydia 'progresses from being a marginal member of a Jewish circle in which she could never receive the covenantal sign, to being a central figure in the local Christian church and the first baptised convert in Europe.'[53] In Philippi there are two households that respond (one a woman's: Lydia, and the other a man's: the Philippian jailer) and it might well be significant that Luke records that Paul and Silas did not go to the jailor's house but to Lydia's once they were released from prison. This could simply be because it was at her home that Paul and Silas had been staying prior to their arrest but commentating from a narrative perspective, Spencer says that the 'scenario suggests Lydia's leadership (headship) role within the local house-church.'[54] Certainly it seems that at least one aspect of the embryonic church met in Lydia's home.

Priscilla and Aquila will be commented on again below, but the reference to them in Acts 18:18-19:1 indicates that during Paul's absence, the work that had been started in Ephesus was left under their care and oversight. It is during this time that they took Apollos aside to explain the way of God to him more accurately.[55]

3.3 Pauline literature: women mentioned by name

In Philippians 4:2-3 Syntyche and Euodia (both women) are described as co-workers. In 1 Corinthians 16:16,18 Paul urges the Corinthians to submit to those who are co-workers and labourers. 'Co-workers' is one of his favoured terms for those who worked with him in the apostolic work of spreading the gospel. The term was used of someone who shared the same trade. So there seems therefore to be evidence that these women had worked alongside Paul in his apostolic task.

---

[53]Witherington, *Women*, p. 216.
[54]Spencer, *Acts*, p. 165.
[55]Spencer, ibid., p. 184, comments that the listing of Priscilla's name before Aquila's in Acts 18:26 suggests 'her primary role as Apollos' teacher.' Further comments on the unusual order of the names will be made below.

In Romans 16 Paul sends greetings to a number of people including women by name. Phoebe is called a deacon (16:1);[56] Priscilla and Aquila are co-workers and are key ministries in the Gentile mission. In the case of this couple Priscilla's name is mentioned before Aquila's probably because she was the more prominent in ministry.[57] Also Junia[58] is described alongside Andronicus as outstanding among the apostles.[59] The most straightforward way of understanding this verse is that she, along with her husband, exercised the ministry of apostle. Chrysostum, writing in the fourth century, says of her, 'Oh how great is the devotion

---

[56]Paul uses the masculine noun *diakonos* and not the feminine verbal participle. If he had used the latter it would be best understood simply as 'servant', but by using the masculine noun it would seem to indicate that she held office in the church in Cenchrea. She is almost certainly the bearer of the letter to the Roman church. Given the number of scholars who have wrestled with Paul's theology in Romans, one wonders if he expected her to explain any unclear issues to the Roman Christians!

[57]They are mentioned 6 times in the NT, on four of the occasions her name comes first. Given that the first time they are mentioned in Acts Aquila's name comes first (which would be in line with custom) we note that statistically it is highly significant that her name appears first. There are only two options: the one suggested in the text above, or that she came from a higher socially significant background. In the light of the NT condemnation of giving weight to status this is highly unlikely. John Chrysostum is quoted in Charles Trombley, *Who Said Women Can't Teach* (South Plainfield: Logos, 1985), p. 29, as commenting on the order of the names, saying, 'the wife must have had, I think, greater piety than her husband. This is not simple conjecture; its confirmation is evident in the Acts.'

[58]Although the NIV translates this as Junias (a male name) this is in fact very unlikely. It is just possible that Junias is a contraction of the Roman (masculine) name Junianus but this is actually unknown. Otherwise, Junia is a very common woman's name. One manuscript actually gives the name as Julia: probably a scribal error but at least it further points toward seeing the name as feminine. See the comments by James Dunn, *Romans 9-16*, Word Commentary Series (Waco, TX: Word, 1991), p. 894. He quotes Lampe as indicating over 250 examples of 'Junia', none of 'Junias'.

[59]The most straight-forward way of understanding this phrase is that they were apostles in their own right, rather than they were well known to the apostolic band. See Dunn, ibid., pp. 894f.

of this woman that she should be counted worthy of the appellation of apostle.'[60] Other women Paul mentions in this chapter are: Mary, Tryphaena, Tryphosa, Persis and Julia.

In Colossians 4:15 Paul speaks of the church that met in Nympha's house which probably indicates that she had some leadership role within that church. Overall, the impression given in the Pauline writings is that there were a variety of women involved in the work of the church.[61]

3.4 Paul: The ultimate egalitarian text of Galatians 3:28

'There is neither Jew nor Greek, slave nor free, male nor female, for you are all one in Christ Jesus', stands for all time as a summary of the equality in Christ. The gospel was good news — particularly if one was non-Jewish, a slave or a woman. (Perhaps the gospel was bad news for those who were Jewish, male and rich: access to God was no longer their sole right!)

It is not possible to maintain that this verse only relates to the status of men and women before God with no relevance to the horizontal outworking of this new status. The whole purpose of Paul's theological argument in Galatians is to deal with a *social and relational* problem. It would appear that the background is that certain Judaisers want to insist on the Gentile converts taking on board the whole Jewish law if they are to be recognised as Abraham's children. Until they do they cannot relate to Jewish believers on an equal basis. Hence the problem is both theological — who are the children of God / Abraham? And sociological — can both groups relate together? Paul in arguing

---

[60]Evans, *Woman*, p. 124, quoting *The Homilies of St John Chrysostum*, Vol. 11, p. 555.

[61]Witherington, *Women*, pp. 188f., suggests that the term 'in the Lord' which is applied to some of the women Paul mentions by name likely means 'in the church' when used in this context, thus meaning that these are women who are ministries in the church.

theologically drives home the point that equality before God must mean nothing less than relational equality between previously divided groups. Robert Wall summarises it this way,

> In Galatians Paul develops his argument for justification by faith in order to correct a social problem: Gentile believers have been excluded from fellowship with Jewish believers because they did not observe the law. Paul demonstrates that justification by faith means that Gentile believers are included within the people of God; on the basis of this doctrine Gentile believers have the right to eat at the same table with Jewish believers.[62]

This verse therefore gives us key insight on the new humanity that is found in Christ, and has profound implications for the church. Consisting of redeemed humanity, the church must ensure that it is modelling the values of the coming kingdom.[63]

Although most translations simply translate all the phrases as 'neither... nor' (e.g. NIV as quoted above) Paul actually negates the male/female distinction in very radical terms. Translated literally he says that there is, 'not male and female' in Christ. In some way the male/female distinction that we find in creation (God created them 'male and female') no longer applies to those who are in Christ. In Christ even the creation order (if there is a defined one) is transcended.

He develops a similar argument in 1 Corinthians 11 (a so-called difficult passage) when he says that, 'in the Lord, however, woman is not independent of man, nor is man independent of woman' (1 Cor. 11:11). Although Paul argues for the distinctiveness of men and women

---

[62]Robert Wall, *Galatians*, IVP NT series (Leicester / Downers Grove: IVP, 1994), p. 25.

[63]James Dunn, *The Theology of Paul's Letter to the Galatians*, (Cambridge: CUP, 1993), p. 50, drives this home with his statement that 'The language [of Gal. 3:28] implies a radically reshaped social world as viewed from a Christian perspective, equivalent to the 'kingdom-perspective' which informed Jesus' ministry, and with the same eschatological perspective and motivation.'

he places that within the larger context of equality. It is true that he does not allow equality of function to mean that there is no distinction between the genders, but, important for our study, neither does he allow the distinctiveness of the genders to mean inequality of function.

3.5   Concluding remarks

Although, from the material presented thus far, it is not possible to insist that women had equal roles to men within the Christian community, for the biblical texts are simply not conclusive on this matter (e.g., the material on Junia above cannot be claimed to be conclusive, and many texts can be read different ways). However, given the promised activity of the Spirit at Pentecost and the nature of the Pauline gospel, it is to be noted that the expected direction for women would be towards freedom and equality. Indeed outside of the supposed difficult passages there do not appear to be any restrictions that Paul places upon women. He accepts them on his team, he commends them to churches, he founds churches on them, and he even transforms the issue of headship and submission so that women are protected and released to become all they are intended to be.[64]

4.   Jesus, Paul and Women

The cultural background in which Jesus and Paul acted is different to ours and as we proceed to explore some hermeneutical issues it is important that any cultural issues are borne in mind when approaching Scripture. This is not to deny that all passages of Scripture are valid for all *time*, it is simply to state that not all passages of Scripture are valid for all *circumstances*. How eternal truths are applied in one setting might be different to how they are applied in another.

When Jesus is seen against the backdrop of his own culture, he stands out as a radical spokesperson for women and all oppressed

---

[64]The issue of headship and submission as it relates to marriage will be looked at in the next chapter.

people. He elevates women and places demands on his male followers so as men and women can be equally released to follow him. As the Ascended Lord he pours out the Spirit equally on women and men. Again, when Paul is read within the patriarchal culture of his day he too speaks out for women. I intend to show later that any restrictions in Paul can be adequately explained either as corrective measures in order to maintain church order, or for evangelistic reasons. Any restrictions can then be understood to be either purely temporary or local. So I suggest that there is ultimately no contrast between Jesus and Paul.

It is also probably worth noting at this point that there are other mentions of women in ministry beyond Paul. We find that 2 John is addressed to the 'elect lady'. Opinion is varied as to what this term means, however we do know from later church history that the term 'elect person' was used of someone who held office within the church. So it is possible that this refers to a female leader in this church. In Revelation 2:20-23 the woman Jezebel is a major source of problem for the church in Thyatira. The church is not rebuked for allowing a woman to minister, but they are however rebuked because they did not bring discipline to the woman over the means, effect and content of her teaching. (This would have been equally true if she had been a man.)

One thing we can conclude is that the New Testament picture of men and women ministering in the church is considerably different to the conflict we saw in Genesis 3:16. Our next aspect of examination will be a missiological one. We will be looking to see if the egalitarian text of Galatians 3:28 is ever 'compromised' when applied to concrete situations, and, if so, whether there could be good missiological reasons for this.

CHAPTER 4

FOR THE SAKE OF THE GOSPEL

The good news that we can be reconciled to God through Jesus Christ is the most important message that has ever been entrusted to humanity. Paul said that if anything was communicated, even by an angel, that contradicted this good news of freedom, then such a person or being should be eternally condemned (Galatians 1:6,7). Paul himself believed in a gospel that relegated such boundary markers as circumcision to a thing of the past — his gospel was a gospel of freedom. However, when he requested Timothy to join with him he insisted that he was circumcised.[1]

This apparent contradiction (between his general teaching and his specific practice) illustrates Paul's missiological concerns: on the one hand he would not compromise his gospel through the addition of rituals that prolonged the old divisions; on the other hand, he could insist on apparent 'compromise', but only in order that the gospel could be effectively communicated to the people being reached. This 'compromise' enabled communication to take place without causing unnecessary offence.

It is important to grasp this twofold aspect involved to make mission activity successful. The two aspects can appear to be in conflict, as in the illustration from the Paul and Timothy scenario above. In making connection with the Jewish society the missionaries ran the risk that their audience might have understood that Paul really believed in the necessity of circumcision for salvation (in spite of anything he might have

---

[1] See the letter to the Galatians, e.g. ch. 5:1,2 to understand that Paul insisted that Gentile believers did not submit to the Jewish covenant mark of circumcision. Then in Acts 16:1-3 he insists on Timothy being circumcised for the sake of the gospel; Luke recording that this was done to Timothy 'because of the Jews who lived in that area, for they all knew that his father was a Greek'.

said to the contrary, for 'actions speak louder than words'). Yet if he did not insist on Timothy's circumcision the message would never have been listened to. So for communication to take place they had to run the risk of misunderstanding.

Although the word 'compromise' is not a favourite word among those who give authority to Scripture, it is important that this missiological principle is grasped. If mission is to be successful, elements of (apparent) compromise will often be necessary. In mission the church's goal is to reach society with its message of liberation, and to achieve this the church must become incarnated and contextualised into the culture, without ever changing the message that has been entrusted to it. Jesus, who modelled mission for us, became human (thus incarnating or embodying the message) and also first century Jewish human (thus contextualising the message).

The church's missiological task is to build a bridge into the culture, and having made the connection, to transport the gospel across the bridge. To communicate successfully there might well need to be compromise, in the sense of a move away from what is ideal (or in theological terms from what is eschatological); and to communicate faithfully the essential message of the gospel itself must never be compromised. Paul put it this way:

> Though I am free and belong to no man, I make myself a slave to everyone, to win as many as possible. To the Jews I became like a Jew, to win the Jews. To those under the law I became like one under the law (though I myself am not under the law), so as to win those under the law. To those not having the law I became like one not having the law (though I am not free from God's law but am under Christ's law), so as to win those not having the law. To the weak I became weak, to win the weak. I have become all things to all men so that by all possible means I might save some. I do all this for the sake of the gospel, that I may share in its blessings. (1 Corinthians 9:19-23.)

An involvement in mission inevitably involves the church in a very difficult area and if care is not taken, the gospel message itself becomes compromised. If the desire to contextualise becomes the overriding motivation, the church runs the risk of simply becoming another manifestation of the surrounding culture — with the gospel message so hidden that it has lost its distinctive challenge and power. By so doing the gospel itself is compromised in the process.

However, it is also true that the gospel is compromised when no bridge is built into the culture, for the gospel message itself demands that the redeemed community enters the world as Jesus did and become one with the people being reached.

This implies that the task for the church is twofold: the church must be in the world but all world values must be kept out of the church. It can be argued that the more fundamentalist wing of the evangelical church has, at times, been incredibly successful at keeping itself out of the world but allowing world values to dominate within its life — thus sinning twice over in the name of faithfulness to the gospel!

If the church is not incarnated within society it cannot reach it; whereas, if it is so immersed within its culture it will not be present as an alternative to society. As far as understanding the place of women within the New Testament is concerned, one big question is whether there is any evidence that freedom for women was 'compromised' for the sake of the gospel.

Perhaps a current missiological example might help illustrate. Given the general response to women within the Islamic world, a missiologically aware approach would not suggest entering an Islamic arena with a team led by a woman. This would be culturally insensitive and inappropriate — indeed, to do so, could well lead to the gospel itself being discredited. However, if the team simply shaped itself on the basis of mirroring the society it was reaching, the gospel, and its message of freedom, would be compromised to such an extent that the team would be guilty of denying the gospel itself.

A good missiological response means that such a team would act incarnationally and thus within reach of the culture — yet also, to some extent, distanced from the culture to model the freedom that comes through the gospel. The team would be contextualised, but not to the extent that the message was compromised; it would also embody the message, but not in such a way that there was no contact to the society.[2]

We can illustrate the missiological principle as presented in the table below with domination and liberation at the respective ends of the spectrum.[3] The mission body must be true to the liberation of the gospel while reaching into the society through contextualisation. The church as the 'mission body' has the calling to bridge the gap between the specific society and the 'gospel of freedom'.

The society to be reached		The Gospel
Aspects of bondage and domination		Brings liberation and justice to society - breaking all domination
<---- Contextualising	**The mission body must both contextualise and embody the message**	Embodying the truth --->

---

[2] We see this response in Paul. To the Jew he became a Jew (compromise for the sake of the gospel) yet he would not allow his converts to submit to Jewish practices when that meant that the gospel itself would be compromised (see e.g. the message of Galatians).

[3] I suggest that the words 'domination' and 'liberation' are two of the more accurate words to describe both the inner character and resultant impact of, respectively, the world and the kingdom of God. Wink, in e.g. *Engaging the Powers* (Minneapolis: Fortress, 1992), refers to the world as 'the domination system'.

So a response to mission means that the mission body is both incarnated and contextualised within society, yet also seek to draw the society toward the true liberation that is found in Christ. If there is this element within the New Testament with respect to women we would expect the following to be the case:

1) that the place of women within the Christian community was within reach of the surrounding society (contextualised), and that the reason for any 'compromise' was for the sake of the gospel;[4]

2) that women would also experience a greater freedom than was present within society (thus the gospel of freedom being incarnated), with the result that:

3) society was challenged to move toward the freedom expressed by the Christian community.

In examining the possibility that there was a missiological 'compromise' within the New Testament on the place of women, I suggest that a comparative study on slavery and women will be a helpful place to start.

1.   Slavery, women and the gospel

The factors which led to the abolition of slavery are complex, and although Christians were involved in the process it was not simply something which was Christian-led. However, for the Christian

---

[4]Within the NT itself we find women appear to have a greater freedom in the churches in Macedonia and Rome than in Jerusalem and the more Eastern regions — probably reflecting the different degrees of cultural freedom offered women in these different areas. Thus again we recognise that the shape of the Christian community was in part influenced by the surrounding culture.

community there was another major issue involved, namely, what the Bible taught on the issue. This is what makes the Christian response to slavery such an interesting one to compare with the discussion on the place of women within the Christian (and wider) community. In similar fashion the push for freedom for women has not been particularly Christian-led and again the Christian community has had a major issue to face as to what the Bible teaches on the matter.

Christians debated the biblical position on slavery, but essentially what brought conviction that Scripture stood on the side of the abolitionists was the perspective that the gospel brought. The gospel as a message of liberation was the ultimate conviction that Bible believing Christians were right in standing for abolition. Such an institution was no longer seen to be compatible with the belief that all people were equal before their creator. In the light of the gospel, freedom meant that an appropriate outworking should take place in the sphere of social relationships, and therefore emancipation was understood to be the right course of action.

When the Bible itself was examined Scripture was seen to contain a strong internal critique of slavery. Although at face value biblical verses seemed to endorse slavery, the overwhelming thrust of freedom and equality before God of all individuals meant that (literally) enslaving Scriptures were eventually swept aside as no longer applying in modern culture.[5]

---

[5] See the discussions in Willard Swartley, *Slavery, Sabbath, War and Women* (Scottdale: Herald Press, 1983), and in Kevin Giles, 'The Biblical Argument for Slavery: Can the Bible Mislead' in *The Evangelical Quarterly*, Vol. LXVI, No. 1 (Jan, 1994). The heart of the pro-slavery argument came down to five key points: 1) slavery was established by God; 2) it was practised by righteous people; 3) the moral law (perhaps an inaccurate term, but what was meant by this was the law as summarised in the 10 commandments) sanctioned and regulated slavery; 4) Jesus accepted slavery; and 5) the apostles upheld it. It was J.B. Lightfoot in his commentary on Philemon that seems to have been the first scholar to suggest

The situation with regard to women is very similar. It is worth expanding slightly on this issue of the 'internal critique' for the situation with women is very similar. (In fact I suggest that the 'internal critique' is even stronger in the case of women, than in the situation over slavery.)[6] Slavery, it was claimed, was grounded in the (moral) law and (perhaps) even on the teachings of Jesus (1 Tim. 6:1-3). In short, the argument was made that equality was a myth for some had been gifted to lead while others were to follow, thus slavery was not an inappropriate institution. Yet there was an 'internal critique' of slavery. Even slavery within Israel, which was of a kinder variety than was found in the surrounding cultures, meant that someone belonged to someone else, but the Scriptures (as a whole) taught that people bear the image of God and therefore must be treated as subjects and should not be reduced to the objects owned by someone else. Those who traded in slaves were specifically condemned (1 Timothy 1:10; Revelation 18:13) and in the situation with Philemon's slave, Onesimus, Paul sought to see him restored to Philemon as more than a slave (Philemon 16,17). It was these specific texts and the general direction of Scripture that encouraged Christians of a later era to go beyond direct biblical instructions and endorse abolition. Abolition was understood as being the position that best lined up with the overall teaching of the Scriptures and was the clear implication of the freedom that comes with the gospel of Jesus Christ. (I wonder how many of us struggle over the biblical teaching on slavery, and in the light of that whether future generations

---

that although the Bible allowed slavery that the principles for its eventual overthrow were laid down in Paul and the gospel (see Giles, p.5).

[6] It is this issue of internal critique (also known as the intra-canonical debate) that makes advancing a case for the acceptance of same-sex practice a difficult one. Those who wish to endorse such a view and also accept the Bible as authority would have to show that there was biblical evidence that pointed in an opposing direction to the Scriptures that condemn such a practice. It is from this hermeneutical principle that this issue is in direct contrast to the biblical witness with respect to slavery and to women.

will also simply gloss over biblical passages that seem to restrict women.)

In due course we will look at the 'household codes' (Scriptures such as Ephesians 5:22 etc., where Paul outlines appropriate relational codes within the household) but it is worth noting that he does not use the terms 'rule' and 'obey' when he writes about the relationship between husbands and wives. He transforms patriarchy (society where men rule) rather than simply endorses it, defining headship not in terms of rule, but as costly self-sacrifice. It could be argued that he was less radical with slaves for he tells them to 'obey' their masters. Certainly the internal critique against patriarchy is at least as powerful as the internal critique of the institution of slavery.

If this is so, we need to take care that we do not find ourselves in a position that emulates that of the pro-slavery evangelicals of the nineteenth century who sought to defend the authority of Scripture while failing to grasp the implications of the gospel of freedom.[7]

1.1   Slavery, women and the 'household codes'

The traditionalist[8] maintains that the comparison between the biblical teaching on slavery and on women/wives is an unfair comparison as one is based on a social relationship, the other on a creation ordinance. So Hurley states, 'The New Testament treats parent/child and husband/wife relations as ordained of God. Nowhere, however, does it suggest the same for slavery', and 'Paul does not endorse slavery, but rather

---

[7]Consider Charles Hodge's comments that, 'If the present course of the abolitionists is right, then the course of Christ and the apostles were wrong' (from *Cotton is King*, p. 849, quoted in Swartley, *Slavery*); or the 1835 declaration by the Presbyterian synod of West Virginia which stated that abolition was a dogma contrary to 'the clearest authority of the word of God' (quoted in Giles, 'Argument', p.12).

[8]I use this term to describe the viewpoint of those who hold to a subordinate role for women.

regulates it and indicates its undesirable nature.'[9] Grudem and Piper likewise dismiss the comparison, saying that 'the similarity is superficial and misguided'.[10] In due course we will look at this perspective to see if their words are justified. First, though I want to examine areas of similarity and then look at the 'household codes' in the New Testament to see if they were intended to be structures set in place for all time.

1.1.1 The household codes (often called 'haustafeln')[11]

Codes defining how relationships were to be structured were very common in the ancient world, and the New Testament also presents codes which were closely modelled on those of secular society.[12] We could define these biblical codes as 'ethical duties which are addressed to specific classes of people specifying for them conduct that befits Christians in everyday life.'

One of the big questions that has been raised is how do the household codes, with an emphasis on submission, fit alongside the egalitarian Scriptures (ones which advocate freedom) of Galatians 3:28 and Colossians 3:11? If all are equal before Christ why is there an emphasis on the submission of specific people to others? On the issue of slavery, it is interesting to note that the pro-slavery argument was simple: slaves were equal as far as acceptance before God was concerned, but as human equality is a myth, the institution of slavery is God-ordained, so as those who are gifted to lead can lead, and those who are inferior can find their fulfilment in being slaves to those who are superior. Those

---

[9]James Hurley, *Man and Woman in Biblical Perspective* (London: IVP, 1981), p. 159.

[10]Grudem & Piper (eds.), *Manhood*, p. 66.

[11]The material in Keener, *Paul*, pp. 131-224, and Padgett, 'The Pauline Rationale for Submission: Biblical Feminism and the *hina* Clauses of Titus 2:1-10' in *The Evangelical Quarterly*, Vol. LIX, No. 1, (Jan. 1987), can be consulted to develop this discussion further. The German term 'haustafeln' is often used by theologians to describe these household codes.

[12]The fullest one is in Ephesians 5:21-6:9; there are also other occurrences of these codes in a less formalised and often shortened structure in other passages.

who argued this way wanted to believe that they could endorse slavery without denying equality; those who took an abolitionist stance wanted to abolish slavery without denying the need for leadership through gifting. This is a very similar situation we find ourselves in today over the case of women in leadership. Those who deny women the possibility of being leaders accept that women are equal, but insist that men have been appointed to lead — male leadership should then be exercised in a way that does not deny women equal status before God. Those who advocate the acceptance of women in leadership propose that to deny a gifted woman the right to serve in leadership is also to deny that she is equal to a man.

The household codes were part of ancient culture and it was Aristotle (fourth century BC) who introduced three pairs of relationships into the household codes; all of which were addressed to the man. He was addressed as a husband (husband/wife relationship); as a father (father/children); and as a master (master/slave). The man was addressed because he was the one who had the authority in these relationships. This threefold format was then adopted by other writers.

Roman aristocracy felt that their power base was being increasingly threatened by social changes around them. The upward mobility of socially inferior elements (former slaves, foreigners and women) was seen as a great threat. Foreign religions, in particular, were seen to be one of the main problems and the turning of a wife from her husband's religion was seen as a subversive ploy on the part of these foreign religions.

> A wife ought not to make friends on her own, but to enjoy her husband's friends in common with him. The gods are the first and most important friends. Wherefore it is becoming for a wife to worship and to know only the gods that her husband believes in, and to shut the door tight upon all queer rituals and outlandish

superstitions. For with no god do stealthy and secret rites performed by a woman find any favour.[13]

Because foreign religions were viewed suspiciously in Rome, writers such as Josephus used the normal model of the household code to allay the suspicions of the Romans. He was at pains to show that Judaism was not a religion that would undermine Rome, but rather enhance Roman society. Josephus made use of the household code model for apologetic reasons, using the threefold division of those codes to demonstrate to Roman society how orthodox the Jewish people were in family practice.

Paul uses the exact same threefold division that was common to secular society and I believe a very strong case can be made to show that he also employs the codes for apologetic reasons (although it needs to be acknowledged that this does not necessarily mean that the instructions are *purely* there for apologetic reasons). He uses the household code model as a defence for Christianity so as it could gain a better hearing in Roman society.

1.1.2 For evangelistic reasons

Paul (or a disciple) emphasised a number of relationships and how they should be conducted in Titus 2. In that chapter he indicates he wants order in relationships particularly for the sake of the gospel. This consistently comes through in the passage (2:1-10). He addresses the

---

[13]Plutarch quoted in Keener, *Paul*, p. 142. This does not mean that the only element involved in these instructions are for apologetic reasons, for it is clear that, e.g., young men should be self controlled as that is appropriate behaviour - we could not argue that such instruction was some form of compromise! However, the apologetic framework means that we should not feel bound that there is, e.g., only one model of marriage based on Paul's words in Ephesians 5:22. We might feel that the comparison he makes between Christ and the church with the husbands relationship to his wife does indicate that male headship is the only model, but we could not simply argue that from the household code *structure*.

behaviour of: women 'so that no-one will malign the word of God' (v. 5); young men 'so that those who oppose you may be ashamed because they have nothing bad to say about us' (v. 8); and slaves 'so that in every way they will make the teaching about God our Saviour attractive' (v. 10). We find a similar emphasis in 1 Timothy 6:1 in the context of masters and slaves, who are to behave in a befitting way toward each other 'so that God's name and our teaching may not be slandered'. Likewise, Peter addresses wives and their behaviour toward their husbands 'so that if any of them do not believe the word, they may be won over without words' (1 Pet. 3:1).

Paul, the believer in freedom, advocated that believers should not use their freedom for their own ends but for the sake of the gospel. True Christian freedom meant that he himself was willing to become obedient to authorities for the sake of the gospel (1 Corinthians 10:31-33), and also willing to become all things to all people (1 Corinthians 9:19- 23).

Seen against this apologetic background certain ethics within these household codes can be understood as 'not a falling away from the Pauline position but the working out of what it means to be saved in the midst of the world.' If there are elements within these household codes that fall short of the gospel of freedom they can be seen as 'the temporary marching orders for the church, so that the gospel could go forth.'

The household codes then fit the pattern of contextualisation that one would expect in a mission-minded person such as Paul. However, he does not simply accept the norms of society for he also considerably adapts the household codes.

1.1.3 The transformation of the household codes

If Paul used the framework of the household codes for apologetic reasons, we also note that he radically transformed the content of those codes. He never advocated that believers compromised their freedom to the extent of secular society. The equality that was theirs through the gospel was not to be completely thrown away.

Unlike the secular codes, he avoids using the terms 'obeying' and 'ruling' with regard to wives and husbands. He is happy to use the term 'submission', for such behaviour should characterise all Christians, and therefore was totally appropriate behaviour for a wife. He also sets the submission of the wife in a context: an immediate context of mutual submission (Ephesians 5:21) and an overall context of being filled with the Spirit (Ephesians 5:18).[14] And unlike the secular codes, he also addresses both parties: thus he refuses to endorse the idea that only the husband had authority.

The content Paul places in the codes indicate how radical he is. He fills them with love and service, each party to the other, in such a way that the codes are radically transformed. Submission does not become the duty of the wife alone, any more than love is only required of the man! Far from defining headship in terms of rule and authority, he draws upon the model of Christ's self-sacrificial giving.[15] He instructs the

---

[14]Grudem & Piper (eds.), op. cit., pp. 198-201, suggest that 'submission to one another' does not mean mutual submission, but that it is an overall phrase talking of submission within relationships, that are then explained by the examples that Paul proceeds to give. By so doing they indicate that, in their opinion, husbands should not be in submission to their wives. This interpretation of 'one another' would be very different to every other occurrence of it within Paul — including the immediate context of speaking to one another (verse 19). The worship and the submission all flow directly out of being filled with the Spirit. The relationships are governed not by some form of hierarchy but by the believers' 'reverence for Christ'.

[15]Although Christ is Lord over the church, it is not this aspect of Christ's relationship to the church that Paul compares to the relationship of the husband to the wife. We must not push the illustration beyond where Paul intended it. We cannot, for instance, draw the bizarre conclusion that the husband is divine and the wife is not. The husband/wife relationship should mirror that of Christ and the church on this issue of partnership with the husband seeking to emulate the self-sacrificial love of Jesus. Using the term 'head' does not justify the husband in lording it over his wife.

wife to recognise her husband as her head and submit; the man, he instructs, to recognise that this description of head is a call to sacrificial love and service on behalf of his wife. By fulfilling such instructions there will be a mutuality, a true unity (Ephesians 5:31).

So although he uses the household code pattern for apologetic reasons, he so fills them with Christian content that the only way they can be outworked successfully is to be filled with the Spirit, embracing a spirit of humility and submission to one another. To use such household codes to establish a divinely appointed order of hierarchy would be to ignore both the spirit and content of those codes. For the husband to demand his right to rule would be to act in an un-Christian way; for the wife to seek to get her way would be to dishonour the One who bought her. Paul is not endorsing male hierarchy, nor even encouraging equal rights — rather he is insisting that believers lay down their rights for one another. The passage then is not about equal rights but about mutual submission.

If Paul can ask slaves to submit without supporting slavery then surely he can ask wives to submit without supporting male dominance. By examining the historical context and the Christian content of the household codes it is very clear that Paul is transforming culture while maintaining an apologetic approach for the sake of the gospel.

Where does that leave things as far as leadership within the home is concerned? That is the challenge that Paul leaves the Christian couple with. The mystery of Christ and the church is that only in partnership with the church is Christ going to get his will done. The church and Christ remain distinct, but what Christ has done is for the church (Ephesians 1:21-23) so that the will of God might be done through the church (Ephesians 3:10). If domineering male headship is resorted to there is a falling short from the partnership that God intends, with husband and wife demonstrating one flesh unity. To fall back to such a position is to move from where Paul would have us focus. He focuses both husband and wife on the Spirit's enabling, Christ's presence and Christ's example, so that each might adopt a self-sacrificial life on behalf the other. To resort to a hierarchy might, at times, be necessary but in reality only indicates our immaturity. The household codes, as laid out by Paul, are not simply secular codes that have been revamped: they are Christian codes. By accepting them as an enduring example of self-giving submissive attitudes, God will be honoured. However, we cannot use them to insist on a hierarchy.

Excursus: Household codes and 'creation order'

It is worth noting that Paul never appeals to creation order as the basis of submission. The context for the household codes is apologetic (for the sake of the Gospel) but the content is modelled on Christ himself. With regard to male/female relationships, Paul only appeals to creation in 1 Corinthians 11:8f. and in 1 Timothy 2:12ff. In the Corinthian passage he is quick to make sure that we do not carry his argument too far by emphasising that 'in the Lord, however, woman is not independent of man, nor is man independent of woman'. So even when resorting to creation he is quick to prevent his readers from deriving too much from his argument.[16]

End of Excursus

1.1.4 The freedom of Galatians 3:28

Paul adopts the well-known form of the household codes for apologetic reasons, and in doing so it can appear that he 'compromises' his gospel of freedom. We do, however, see Paul working out his gospel of freedom and equality in different contexts. He addresses Jew and Gentile unity in the Galatian context; men and women having equal rights in 1 Corinthians 11:2-16; the reciprocal authority within marriage in 1 Corinthians 7:1-5; the slavery issue with Philemon (who is to receive

---

[16]For a discussion on the Corinthian passage and in particular to the historic style of Paul's argument see Keener, *Paul*, pp. 19-69. We will examine the Timothy passage in chapter 6.

Onesimus back no longer as a slave, but as a brother (Philemon 16))
and also in the household code in his letter to the Ephesians, where he
instructs masters to 'treat your slaves in the same way'.

Summary

Paul is radical in how he applies Christ's freedom to the relationships of
his day. He uses great apologetic wisdom by employing the accepted
household codes of his society, but he refuses to adopt cultural norms.
He particularly transforms the relationship between husbands and wives,
and masters and slaves. His radical demands mean that he has sown the
seeds that will eventually dismantle the institution of slavery and, it would
seem, the ultimate demise of patriarchy in church structure and
relationships. Anything less will be less than Christian.

It can be debated whether Paul would have envisaged any other
model than the husband as head of the wife (and therefore some form of
patriarchy) and it is certainly possible that he did not envisage total
freedom for women. This could be either because he was focused on
the apologetic issues or he himself did not grasp the full implication of the
gospel. (We might also want to speculate whether he really envisaged
that the gospel was in conflict with slavery as an institution.)

As far as the household codes are concerned I suggest that we
have three possibilities that would all push us to a position of freedom
and equality for women. 1) That there is a measure of compromise
present but because of Paul's apologetic focus; 2) that the household
codes actually present a position of total freedom, there being no
compromise within them when understood correctly; or 3) that once the
Pauline instructions are taken to their logical conclusion we would arrive
at a position of equality. It is with the first and third positions above that
a position beyond the Pauline one would be advocated. With the first
position we would simply be re-contextualising the gospel for our culture
and era, and in that sense would not be going beyond Scripture, while
with the third position we would explicitly be going beyond the text of
Scripture. However, this is surely what was done by Christians with

respect to the slavery issue (and as we will examine in the next chapter there is another issue being raised in all this, which is to do with the meaning of living under the authority of Scripture).

It is now that we turn to the argument put forward that there is a very big difference between the example of slavery and the marriage relationship. It is interesting that the current argument (that there is a difference of order between these two sets of relationships) is to insist on something which the pro-slavery group did not understand. They understood that any undermining of the master/slave relationship automatically would mean that male leadership was also undermined. They saw the two sets of relationship as directly parallel to each other. It is to this discussion that we now turn.

1.2   Slavery is cultural; male / female relationships are creational

There are those who argue that the similarity between the emancipation of slaves and freedom for women is superficial. One is reflective of fallen culture; the other is reflective of creation order. Slavery is to do with social order; submission of women/wives is to do with the way God intended things to be.[17] The argument continues that any idea of mutual submission is nonsense for parents are not told to submit to their children, thus what we find outlined in Ephesians are fixed relationships.

In reply I point out that the wife/husband relationship is set in the context of mutual submission (Ephesians 5:21), and to take Paul's language any other way is to distort the plain Pauline and contextual meaning of the phrase. Likewise he brings a reciprocal element into the master/slave relationship by instructing masters to 'treat your slaves the same way' (Ephesians 6:9). However, he makes no such requirement

---

[17]It is noted that nowhere are women told to submit to men; nor that men are head over women. The term 'head' is only ever used in a marriage context. If there is to be any specific subordination it can therefore only be restricted to marriage. This is a point that those who advocate the hierarchical position consistently fail to grasp.

within the parent/child relationship. He does not set these three sets of relationships on equal terms, but what is clear is that it is the master/slave relationship, rather than the parent/child relationship, that is treated as closer in analogy to that of husband/wife.

The reasons for submission in ancient society were: inferior power, economic dependence and less knowledge. In ancient society this meant that it was to the man that all submitted — wives, children and slaves. For this reason the traditional household codes only addressed the men. Children come under a very different category to that of slaves and wives, both latter categories consisting of adults and so capable of a measure of independent survival. It would be ludicrous for Paul to insist on mutual submission for parents and children; this not only goes against divine order but common sense!

The real issue is not whether marriage is a God-ordained relationship and slavery is not. Indeed, there are really two issues at stake here: first, what kind of marriage is God-ordained? Is it simply one of submission one-way? From Paul's teaching, the Genesis picture pre-fall, and the emphasis on unity within marriage, such a view would be hard to substantiate. The second, and very key, issue is to discover in what sense the coming of Christ has actually transformed creation. Redemption does not simply restore creation to how it was. In Christ creation finds its destiny fulfilled, it reaches its end in the one who is the Beginning and the End. Christ is the Last Adam and as such has come to inaugurate a new humanity that is manifest even within this fallen age. We might not yet be like him, but in Christ there is no male and female.[18]

Slavery and marriage are of a different order. However domination and hierarchy are of the same order. They belong to the order that is passing away, believers are to live in a way that models the coming age of glory.

---

[18]I suggest that in Gal. 3:28 Paul uses the term 'not male *and* female' quite deliberately.

2.   Marriage and order

Although this is not a book on marriage, in the light of using the household codes as an example of relationships being ordered for apologetic reasons, it is worth giving some indication as to how the marriage relationship should be ordered.

As far as men and women in relationship together is concerned, it is only in the marriage relationship that we find women are asked to submit to their husbands. This occurs in the context of the household codes which we understand to be, at least in part, apologetically motivated. This raises the question whether we have in them a fixed order for all time.

In Ephesians 5:22-33 Paul does not argue for a fixed order on the basis of creation but does compare the husband/wife relationship to that of Christ and the church. This might indicate some sort of divine order in marriage. If so, however, the model is not one of domineering but of self-sacrificial giving, and the goal of the relationship is harmonious unity.

What is important in marriage is for both partners to agree on their concept of headship as they enter marriage. A gentle form of male headship is suggested by Dennis McCallum and Gary DeLashmutt, that makes for a reasonable starting point for discussion within marriage. They suggest that,

> A woman who submits to the servant leadership of a mature Christian man should be letting herself in for a life where her husband devotes himself to providing for her needs, protecting her and (yes) directing her at times. A servant leader will not insist on his way where it is not possible to know objectively what God wants. He will call for his wife to follow Christ along with himself, but will graciously allow her to refuse his

suggestions often. Like Jesus, he will not compel obedience, but will seek to win it through persuasion and love.[19]

Alongside mutual submission in marriage, the ideal is that no marriage should be closed to the comments of, and help from, other members of the body of Christ that a couple are in relationship with. When a husband and wife end up unable to resolve an issue themselves it is best to invite others in to help resolve the best way forward. If agreement still can't be reached, McCallum and DeLashmutt suggest it is the husband's prerogative to hold through for his view, or to choose to sacrificially yield to his wife's view. (Assuming that neither choice can be labelled 'sin'.) The decision by the husband in leading or in yielding must be done with a wholehearted commitment to the marriage by both husband and wife.

3.   For the sake of the gospel

Having looked at the ordering of relationships within the New Testament and the household codes in their historic setting, I suggest there is evidence that women were sometimes restrained from giving total expression to the freedom that was theirs in Christ. This was not from a theological basis grounded in the creation narratives, thus indicating an inequality between the genders, but only for apologetic reasons. Hence in applying Scriptures that seem to restrict women,[20] or ones that give a fixed order of men and women relating together (as seen in the household codes), we should not feel that they are binding in exactly the way laid out. For them to be binding they would need to clearly reflect creation order, the freedom of the gospel and be completely free of any apologetic or corrective element.

---

[19]From 'Men, Women and Gender Roles in Marriage' a paper adapted from their *The Myth of Romance* (Minneapolis: Bethany, 1996), and released on the Web site [http://www.xenos.org/ books/mythmw.htm].

[20] The three main Pauline ones will be examined in chapter 6.

A. F. Johnson has caught this aspect when he suggests that just as God's word would have been dishonoured in New Testament times by wives not submitting to their husbands, it is dishonoured today when outsiders come into a male-dominated church that seems to suppress women.[21] In other words, as for Paul, we must be apologetically motivated as we seek to implement the freedom that Christ has purchased, and should be aware that the outworking of that freedom will differ from culture to culture.

In closing, I would like to deal with one concern that is often raised. It is sometimes suggested that those who advocate freedom for women are simply following the lead given by the world.[22] I suggest this needs to be responded to in two ways. First, we need to acknowledge that God is sovereign and therefore is at work in the world. If it was secular society that first raised its voice regarding freedom for women, this does not necessarily indicate that God was not involved in this concern. Second, the issue remains that once a concern has been raised (whether inside or outside the church) that Jesus is the one who is followed. In other words, society can raise an issue (another example might be that of ecology) but the redeemed community must then determine whether God is speaking and what it means to follow Christ.

So in the example of ecology, I suggest that Christians should not be responding because we are in danger of running out of resources, but because this is God's earth and we are to take care of it. Society might have 'flagged' the issue, but we then need to follow Christ. The same might have been true with respect to women. As Christians we must model what he taught on equality, rather than simply adopt society's agenda.

---

[21]'Response' in *Women, Authority & the Bible*, Alvera Mickelsen (ed.) (Downers Grove: IVP, 1986), p. 157.
[22]I will return to this concern specifically in chapter 8.

This chapter has opened up a key hermeneutical issue, that, for the sake of the gospel, certain freedoms might well be best restricted. The next chapter will address other hermeneutical issues. In reality, hermeneutical issues are at the centre of the debate over the place of women in society and the church. It is not simply *what* the various texts say, but *why* they say what they say, and *how* they should be applied in our setting, that determines the way forward.

CHAPTER 5

READING THE BIBLE

In the previous chapter, we considered the comparative nature of the biblical instructions to slaves and to women. Our conclusion was that there is a valid comparison between them. As far as slavery is concerned, the overwhelming opinion is that in order for us to act Christianly, we would need to oppose slavery as an institution, in spite of the biblical texts that seem to endorse it. In other words, to be biblical we need to go beyond simply quoting biblical verses. This approach has always been recognised as necessary on all theological issues, otherwise we might become involved in a practice such as baptising believers on behalf of those who have died (1 Corinthians 15:29), or we could advocate that certain people literally removed their own eyes (Matthew 5:29).

One of the central issues in the debate over the appropriate place for women is, without doubt, a hermeneutical one. Claire Powell in a succinct article,[1] highlights some of the key elements in the hermeneutical debate, some of which I will repeat. Some hermeneutical issues, such as how best to understand the creation narratives, or how to read the household codes in the light of their cultural setting, have already been considered, and I do not intend to repeat those arguments in this chapter. However, with the previous discussions in mind I will seek to draw together some hermeneutical keys that will lay a foundation before looking at the texts that seem to restrict women's roles.

---

[1] 'A stalemate of genders? Some hermeneutical reflections' in *Themelios*, Vol. 17.3 (April / May, 1992), pp. 15-19.

1.   Hermeneutical keys

1.1 Recognise the inadequacy of a 'flat book' approach

There is a tendency among those who understand the Bible to teach a restriction on women and their roles, to use the Bible in a particular way. This method is often described as a 'flat book' approach. By this phrase, it is meant that there is a greater emphasis placed on quoting what the Bible says irrespective of the culture or other factors. The cumulation of texts can then be used to prove the particular point. This was the approach that was used to defend the right of Christians to have slaves: effectively what was argued was that they had Scripture on their side.

The danger of this approach can lead us to the place where institutions are defended because they are in the Bible, although the nature of the institution itself can be seen to fall short of the human interrelationships that the gospel envisaged. So although at first appearing biblical, it leads to a misuse of the Bible. It is for this reason that I suggest we need to place greater weight on the activity of Jesus and the freedom that results from the deliverance the gospel brings.

1.2 Recognise that historical and cultural settings are important

It is important that weight is given to the background setting of the texts we are dealing with. Again, the slavery debate is a useful one to cite as it illustrates this principle so well. Those who stood for the abolition of slavery argued that slavery was part of ancient culture and that the law did not endorse slavery as such, but rather the law accepted the situation as a fact of society but then moved the culture for the covenant people toward protection and freedom for slaves. The law did not abolish slavery but improved the situation. However, given a new setting, the only appropriate Christian way forward was to endorse abolition.

Paul, and Pauline texts, are rightly given a great deal of weight among those who give the Bible authority on doctrine and practise, but it is important to note that Paul's letters were not written as creedal statements or works of systematic theology. All of his letters were dependent on the situation he was writing to. This is not to say that the contingent nature of the letters means that they do not contain theology, but to recognise that they were written to a specific situation at a specific time. It could be argued that, for instance, the letters to the Ephesians and Romans could be exceptions to this principle of contingency. Even the letter to the Romans which is without doubt the most concentrated letter on Pauline theology, with such a clear exposition of his gospel, is still in measure contingent. There seems to be at least two main reasons: he has not been in Rome and wants to communicate to them the essence of his gospel and, a much more contingent reason, he wants to address the issue of Jews and Gentiles relating together, which appears to have been a particular issue at Rome. Hence his presentation of the gospel is shaped to address that issue. The letters therefore need to be seen against their primary context and then, if necessary, re-contextualised for ours. This factor is what lay behind F. F. Bruce's response to the question, 'How do you interpret 1 Timothy 2:9-15, which suggest that women are not to teach?' His entire recorded reply was, 'It is merely a statement of practice at a particular time.'[2] This author of over 40 books could dismiss these verses so quickly because of the specific context that Paul was addressing. Therefore he could not accept these verses as having universal application.

To state that all biblical passages are for all time, does not mean that all biblical passages are for all circumstances. In the case of the Timothy passage mentioned above, we would want to discover the factors involved in Paul's statement in order to learn from the apostle, rather than making it into a universal restriction against women teaching.

---

[2]This interview of Bruce by W. Ward Gasque and Laurel Gasque was entitled 'F. F. Bruce: A Mind for What Matters' and appeared in *Christianity Today* (April 7, 1989), pp. 22-25.

1.3 Recognise that unclear texts should be interpreted in the light of clear ones

Each of the key restrictive passages present the interpreter with specific challenges. Powell says that they 'are significantly among the most difficult in the NT, including a number of *hapax legomena* and verses such as 1 Timothy 2:15, which still awaits a really convincing exegesis.'[3] In the case of the verses that tell women not to talk in the church (1 Corinthians 14:34-36) there is the further complication as to whether these verses were ever intended to be part of the canonical writings at all!

These comments should temper a statement such as that made by Stephen Clark who chooses 1 Timothy 2:8-15 as an interpretative centre on the question of appropriate roles for women. He writes, '1 Timothy 2:8-15 is one of the most important texts to consider in any examination of the New Testament on the roles of men and women.'[4] We can contrast his interpretative centre with that of F. F. Bruce who places Galatians 3:28 at the centre. He writes, 'Paul states the basic principle here; if restrictions on it are found elsewhere in the Pauline corpus... they are to be understood in relation to Galatians 3:28 and not vice versa.'[5]

In the light of the fact that the key restrictive passages are not as clear as might first appear, Powell draws attention to a text that is seldom referred to in the debate. She notes that there are few references in the debate to 'unequivocal texts such as Colossians 3:16 which clearly states that teaching is the responsibility of all believers. Gender is simply not specified, and neither is it anywhere assumed that some teaching is

---

[3] Powell, 'Stalemate', p. 17. A *hapax legomenon* (Powell has used the plural form) is a term that describes a particular word (in the case of the restrictive texts, a Greek word) that is only used on that one occasion within the NT.

[4] *Man and Woman in Christ* (Ann Arbor, MI: Servant Books, 1990), pp. 191f.

[5] *The Epistle to the Galatians*, New International Greek Testament Commentary, (Exeter: Paternoster Press, 1982), p. 384.

more authoritative than other teaching within the church body, or that a formal sermon slot in church is different from teaching outside a church environment.'[6]

The choosing of clear texts and therefore an interpretative centre is an important factor, as our starting point will in part determine our conclusion. In moving forward we will need the discipline of hearing the apparent conflicting voices that Scripture gives on this particular subject. We must be careful not to silence one of the voices too quickly. Again in making a comparison with the slavery issue, we can note that there are voices that clearly lead us in a different direction to those that seemed to endorse slavery. Paul condemned slave traders (1 Timothy 1:9f.); he sent Philemon back, not only as a slave, but as a brother (Philemon 16); John condemned the traders in Babylon (Rome) who traded in people as well as goods (Revelation 18:13). We would be in grave danger of silencing voices that speak of freedom if we simply amassed restrictive passages together, on slavery or on women.

As well as interpreting unclear texts in the light of clear ones, we need to interpret specific practices in the light of overriding theological and moral principles. This was one of the appeals that those who argued for the abolition of slavery made. If all human beings are created equally in the image of God, they argued, then any institution that allowed for domination or the ownership of someone else had to be seen to be in opposition to the doctrine of God as creator (and redeemer, of course).

1.4 Recognise that we should not make Scripture say more than it does

When we looked at Genesis 2, we have already seen the possibility of making this mistake. For example, to take the word 'helper' to imply

---

[6]Powell, 'Stalemate', p. 17. Although the Col. 3:16 text can be given slants of meaning particularly through different choices of punctuation, thus even making this text less than unequivocal! Thus simply illustrating, yet again, the difficulty in finding texts that all can agree are absolutely clear.

subordination would be to fall into this trap. As far as the key restrictive passages are concerned we need to determine why Paul appeals to creation in 1 Corinthians 11 or 1 Timothy 2. So, in the former passage, his appeal to creation is not to advocate male supremacy but to argue that a woman should be covered.[7] Similarly, although he uses the concept 'head', he does not use this to develop some form of hierarchy or as a means to restrict women in their function. In the latter passage, Paul does not conclude that all women are more easily deceived than men. This could be the reason for the reference to Eve but Paul himself does not specifically state that position. We must resist the temptation of making the text fit any preconceived ideas and we might have to admit that, in the final analysis, we do not know why Paul makes some of his statements. (This is not too unlikely in the light of 2 Peter 3:16!)

1.5 Recognise that teaching texts take precedence over both descriptive and corrective texts

Manfred Brauch, in *Hard Sayings of Paul*,[8] draws attention to three categories of New Testament Scriptures: instructive (or normative) texts, descriptive texts, and corrective texts. The *instructive* texts are those which declare how things ought to be among the followers of Christ. Such texts are didactic and are often based on clear theology related to the redemption that is ours in Christ. *Descriptive* texts describes practices or actions in the church. When these come without any comment they normally accord with the instructive texts. So for example, there is no adverse comment on the ministry of Priscilla and Aquila, nor regarding Philip's four daughters prophesying. If there is unity in Christ and a universal outpouring of the Spirit, regardless of gender, we should expect women to be functioning alongside men. At

---

[7]These texts will be examined in the next chapter. Although it can be argued that Paul is not suggesting the covering of women's heads, I am using that suggestion as a summary of the possibilities.
[8](London: Hodder & Stoughton, 1990), p. 20f. In this classification he is acknowledging a debt to an essay by S. Scott Bartchy.

times a descriptive text has a comment attached, such as we find in the reference to the circumcision of Timothy. This practice seems strange in the light of there being 'no Jew nor Greek' in Christ with circumcision being a boundary marker from the old covenant, so it is most helpful that an explanation is given for this clear exception to the 'rule'. The third category is that of the *corrective* text. These are texts that deal with special situations, problems or misunderstandings within the church, and all the key restrictive passages fit this category. This is not to say that there is no teaching within them, but that any teaching is being specifically applied to a particular situation that needs adjusting.[9] We would have to be very clear indeed to universalise such texts and give them precedence over instructive texts.

I am not implying that we can simply dismiss descriptive or corrective texts as irrelevant, but I am suggesting that they must be subservient to the instructive texts.

1.6 Recognise that we need to apply Scripture consistently

There is a challenge to apply Scripture consistently. If Paul's use of the headship illustration in 1 Corinthians 11 is not advanced to restrict women in ministry but to insist that they cover their heads, we are then left with a question as to what is normative for all ages. Should women today have their heads covered? If we allow women to be present without covering their heads, but restrict them from ministry (and by so doing reverse Paul's instructions, who seems to be insisting that they

---

[9]In some situations corrective texts would, of course, be restoring belief to the norm and therefore such texts would also function as teaching texts (as in the case of Paul's corrective teaching on the resurrection from the dead in 1 Corinthians 15), while in other situations the corrective text might well be addressing a particular situation (perhaps the instruction that there were only 'two or at the most three tongues' per meeting is not a universal instruction). It seems that where practice is being corrected we need to take care in applying such correctives universally. The corrective texts on women seem to be addressing practice more than they are addressing faulty beliefs.

covered their heads but also released them into ministry)[10] we must be clear on the basis for such practise. Philip Payne suggests that, 'It is inconsistent simply to assume on the one hand that it is normative for women never to teach or be in authority over men, but on the other hand to dismiss as not normative Paul's comments about braids, gold, pearls, expensive clothes, and raised hands in prayer.'[11]

If, as most do, we dismiss certain instructions as cultural, but retain others within the same passages as ongoing, we will need a clear hermeneutic to do so. Better rather to see that there is a cultural background to the whole New Testament that colours the various instructions that Paul and others give. This aspect raises an issue which is in part hermeneutical but also belongs to the larger picture relating to the nature of Scripture itself.

2.   An approach to Scripture

There has been an increasing emphasis on the narrative nature of Scripture - with fresh approaches to interpreting Scriptures. I am sure that not all of these approaches will prove to be helpful[12] but the overall emphasis on the Scripture as 'story' will prove a useful way forward. Indeed, in my opinion, it will prove a necessary way forward, for a large percentage of Scripture comes to us in the form of story - narrative rather than laws, oracles or systematic theology. Even where Scripture is not in direct narrative form there is the story line of Scripture that lies behind the text. Indeed behind the sacred texts are the sacred stories

---

[10]This will become clear in the next chapter when we look specifically at this text. Suffice it to note that Paul insists on women covering their heads, but allows them to pray and prophesy. In numerous situations today the instructions are reversed, women can be uncovered but are limited in function.

[11]Philip B. Payne, 'Libertarian Women at Ephesus: A Response to Douglas J. Moo's Article...', *Trinity Journal*, Vol. 2 NS, No. 2 (1981), p. 175.

[12]There is a good article by Gordon Thomas 'Telling a Hawk from a Handsaw? An Evangelical response to the New Literary Criticism' in *The Evangelical Quarterly*, Vol. LXXI / No. 1 (Jan. 1999), pp. 37-50.

which form the very shape of the Jewish and Christian faiths.[13] 'Story' is actually something that is present for all of us, although perhaps unseen.[14] Our worldview is basically our story of what the world is all about. Stories have the power to confirm, inform, instruct, or challenge our worldview(s) and, as a result, our whole lives. Worldviews are shaped through the stories (even nursery rhymes can shape a world view) and the interpretation of events, so much so that the interpretation and re-interpretation of history is always a key issue in shaping a worldview and in forming a society. The history of the British empire can be victorious or disastrous: dependent on how the story is told.

Jesus often told stories (parables) to subvert commonly held perspectives. Before him, Nathan the prophet used the power of story to great effect to open David's life to the presence of God. He told a story of a rich man, a poor man and a little lamb. It was only a story yet the story sufficiently paralleled David's recent misdemeanour that his whole perception was changed.

On the national level, Israel had a story that she re-told in order to bring to remembrance that she was chosen by God from all the nations of the earth; throughout her history she re-told the activities of the heroes who had gone before, they were there to be emulated, and their mistakes were to be avoided. The final editor of Deuteronomy to Kings (the so-called Deuteronomic historian) tells his story from the perspective of Israel as a stiff-necked nation, whose sin is threatening the covenant, and that she is in danger of going into exile. Such a story telling adds up to a radical prophetic call to repent. The story-telling is as

---

[13]See James Sanders, *From Sacred Story to Sacred Text: Canon as Paradigm* (Philadelphia: Fortress, 1987.

[14]I am using the term 'story' here in a technical sense and not in the popular sense of something that is not true. The story of Scripture is a telling of events from a perspective. The events are interpreted to communicate values and shape a world-view.

prophetic as the explicit declarations of judgement that come through such prophets as Amos.

The early church also perceived the power of story. The Old Testament narratives were written to shape *our* lives (1 Corinthians 10:11-12), and behind the NT narratives themselves a story is being told. Jesus, the great story-teller, uses a well-known story of the vineyard: the original story is from Isaiah 5. It is the story of Israel and speaks of the tragedy of her failure to respond to the love of God. Jesus uses this story as the basis for a re-telling (see Matthew 21:33-46; Mark 12:1-12; Luke 20:9-19), and he retells it in such a way that the intensity of the tragedy becomes even more obvious. In the Old Testament, Israel is viewed as the son, yet in the re-telling of this story there is a son who is finally sent to the vineyard. Israel's story is being retold, but the central new character in the story is *the* son. The response to the son is portrayed as the absolute key in the 'success' or indeed failure of Israel to be fruitful in its mission.

An understanding of story is essential as it underlines that the revelation of God is essentially historical and not propositional. Scripture records that there is an unfolding of the revelation of God within the historical experience of God's people. The story reaches it climax, of course, in the revelation that took place in the life and activities of Jesus.

So within Scripture there are stories, and there is also the macro-story that first Israel tells, and then the early church continues to tell but with Jesus having been placed at the centre.

2.1 The five-act play

N. T. Wright gives a very helpful model to understand the unfolding of revelation within the canon of Scripture.[15] Firstly, he establishes that it is

---

[15]The Laing Lecture / the Griffith Thomas Lecture, 1989. The text is published in *Vox Evangelica*, Vol. XXI (1991), pp. 7-32. The model is reproduced in his *The New Testament and the People of God* (Minneapolis: Fortress; London: SPCK, 1992), p. 140f.

God himself who gives to Scripture its authority, and that the Bible is an unfolding of God's activity in different and progressive acts. He gives a helpful analogy of a supposed unfinished five act play of Shakespeare. He asks us to imagine the play as incomplete as the larger part of the final act has been lost. Through this analogy the first four completed acts form the authority for all that follows — the characters must remain consistent with what has already gone before. The first four acts (biblically) are Creation, the Fall, the history of Israel and Jesus. An understanding of the story will then shape the world view of the readers / hearers (or perhaps better the 'viewer' as the story must be seen). Under this model Act 3 would finish with John the Baptist proclaiming that there is one to come who will be the Lamb of God, the baptiser in the Spirit. With bated breath the viewer is asked to watch the fourth act unfold as the God of all creation is revealed in the Person of Jesus. The fourth act then concludes with the death of Christ, with the fifth act opening to the resurrection scene, the outpouring of the Spirit and the mission of the church.

The above acts correspond with the Scriptures as we have them; Scripture substantially ends with the beginning of the fifth act along with some indications as to the end of that act (Romans 8, 1 Corinthians 15, parts of Revelation such as 21-22). The story becomes the authority for all who want to participate in it, and yet it remains incomplete. Using this analogy to introduce people to the larger story, I have commented that such an approach leaves three possible options: 1) to reduce the story we have to the level of interesting ancient literature where a 'museum' (spelt 'church'?) could be erected in honour of the writing. Readings could be made from the book, discussions of its quality and historical credibility could be most informative: yet the dynamic authority of the book would be lost. 2) The 'missing' elements of act 5 could be filled in with authoritative writers who could so fill in the gaps that those who sought to live by the story would know how to act and react in any given situation. However, the people would no longer be on a journey of discovery (and mistake), they would simply be a people of the book and of tradition. 3) The third option is the one that Wright advocates where the church would be 'required to offer an improvisatory performance of the final act as it leads up to and anticipates the intended conclusion'.[16]

If the church is to faithfully improvise it will need to puzzle over the previous acts in order to faithfully tell out the story.[17] The church then inherits the story and must set about its business of restoring to the owner the fruits of his vineyard. The church must immerse itself in the previous acts, for true Christianity cannot simply go and look up a set text to repeat parrot fashion as if it has found the answer. In that sense, right answers cannot be looked up; a good fifth act will not merely repeat what has gone before, but will bring it to a proper completion. Through this model there is also the need for the Spirit to inspire the community to faithfully live out the story that God initiated with creation. A good hermeneutic will require the current actors to faithfully interpret the story of the past and to re-interpret it into the contemporary scene.

Commenting on the authority of the New Testament, Wright gives an excellent summary, stating that:

> In the Bible we find a drama in several acts... But the drama is not over. The way the NT is written is precisely open-ended... with a large blank to be filled in by those who, as the heirs of the final scene in the fifth act, are seeking to advocate the drama, by means of Spirit-led improvisation, towards its appropriate conclusion. The authority of the NT, then, consists not least in this: that it calls us back to this story, this story of Jesus and Paul, as our story, as the non-negotiable point through which our

---

[16]*The New Testament and the People of God*, Fortress / SPCK, 1992, page 142.
[17]Surely this is the meaning of Ephesians 2:10 'we are his artwork' (my translation) and 3:10 'making known to the principalities and powers the manifold wisdom of God'.

pre-history runs, and which gives our present history its shape and direction.[18]

The Old Testament is the story of the earlier acts — giving us vital understanding of what takes place in Act 4 (Jesus). In the light of this, it follows that the Old Testament cannot be the book of the covenant people of God in Christ in the same way that the New Testament is. The New Testament is written as the charter for the people of the creator God in the time between the first and second coming of Jesus (the conclusion of the play). There are boundary markers in the Old Testament which relate to the people of God when they were one nation, one geographical entity, with one racial and cultural identity, and the New Testament builds on the work of God as revealed in the Old Testament. The Old represents the preparatory work but now that the gospel has gone forth universally, it is the New Testament which is the charter for God's people.

Paul and the other first century Christians worked out what it meant for them to be faithful to the story in their day, we must remain faithful to the story in our day. If we tell another story we will become unbiblical — the Bible must operate as the authoritative guide to our story-telling. However it is also true that if we simply repeat scripts from an earlier act, or even an earlier scene within the same act, we will run the risk of becoming unfaithful to the story that God wants told.

Such an approach to Scripture is not only creative but necessary. As far as the subject of women and an appropriate response to them within the Christian community is concerned, we have to ask what is the right response that will accurately tell the story of God's adventure in redeeming humanity. We must determine what shape our Christian community should have if we are to tell the story of the new humanity that Christ has initiated through his death and universal outpouring of his Spirit.

---

[18]*Themelios*, Vol. 16.1, p. 16.

In the previous chapter we considered the possibility that there was 'compromise' within the New Testament for the sake of the gospel. In this chapter I am also suggesting that we need to examine what it means in our day to be faithful to the ongoing story of God's redemption.

Excursus: Is the analogy a suitable one?

There are limitations to all analogies. To talk of an analogy is to say one thing is like something else and by implication to accept that there will also be elements which differ. The issue here is whether the five-act play analogy is an appropriate one and to explore this I wish to highlight the key differences to see if the model falls down.

The main differences are: 1) that the script of a play instructs the actors how to act, but the Bible is a record of what has already been 'acted' out. 2) Within a play all the action is contained in the script, but the Bible cannot claim to contain all of God's activity for God is active outside of the biblical players; he is not simply involved with the redemptive people but is involved in the world. 3) And related to the last comment, a play by definition involves all the characters within it, but making an appeal for the church to improvise does not involve all the characters. God himself and the world are also characters within such a model — the church 'actors' having no control over those 'characters'.

Taking these in order. The first point certainly highlights a significant factual difference, but I question whether it highlights something which undermines the model as a whole. I accept that the script of a play precedes the drama, thus telling the actors what they should say,[19] although it might be argued that it cannot strictly speaking

---

[19]One could argue, at a very literalistic level, that the Scriptural story could indeed be used to inform literal actors what they should say and do to act out what has taken place (thus using Scripture as the foundation of a script for a play), but even within this model the issue of improvisation (or some other means of

tell the actors what they should do. (What the actors do is, to some extent, open to either the characterisation given by the individual actors, or the strong direction of the director.) The difference is not as great as first might be thought and the distance between script and Scripture is exaggerated when we think that a script for a play is produced simply at a textual level and then acted out. Virtually all writings begin at the level of story and ideas and then gradually get worked into a textual form. (Indeed the final published form of some scripts might not even emerge until a season of performances have taken place, as the audience response can be a factor in the final shaping.)

In the model adopted, I am suggesting something much more profound than reducing the Scriptures to a script for a literal play. The biblical play has been acted (and is continuing to be acted) out over a long period of time and on a universal theatre, and what has informed the players who have acted within this play has always been the sacred stories that have been told within those faith communities. Thus the stories that underlie the sacred text of Scripture have acted in exactly the same way as the script does to a play. What we now have, in Scripture, is a record of the script that has been produced. (How else is a script produced other than through the stories that are being told and experienced that are then eventually produced as text?). The differences then are not even so much to do with the means of writing (which is being developed as the actors have acted), but the scale of the production both as far as duration and location is concerned. The analogy, I suggest, then is not too far removed, for given the differences just highlighted, we could imagine a play which has been acted out over a considerable period of time. Let us suggest that it has been put on in the theatre over four evenings with an act per night being shown and that we have now been given the script for the play thus far. We could examine the play and see where the actors have been faithful to the story

---

completing the story) would have to be implemented. Therefore the Scriptures could be used exactly as a script for a play.

and should we be asked to finish the play we would wish to examine the script thus far in order to ensure that the story informed our improvisation which could then (if desired) be later turned into script. That would give us a very close analogy indeed.

The second point raised — that the Bible only contains part of the activity of the drama while a script contains all the activity of a play, I think, again can be responded to in similar fashion. For a play to work it must point beyond itself, and although, as argued, the script of a play contains everything within that particular drama, it does not contain everything that the play is seeking to address, nor does it contain all the stories that have shaped the play. Every script could be expanded to contain more and say more (though sometimes through saying less, more is said), hence every script is selective. This again makes it much closer in nature to Scripture.

The final point was, that in asking the church to improvise is to ignore the other characters in the drama. Thus although the church can be requested to enter the drama there is no corresponding request that could possibly be made to some of the other characters, such as God and the world. However, I suggest that rather than exposing a weakness in the analogy, this actually brings us to the heart of the Scriptural drama. The church cannot control God, but we know that he is faithful to the (redemptive) story line, even if all other actors prove unfaithful. And the world is very much part of the drama. Indeed the world is faithful to its story line as it acts out its fallen character. Whatever 'improvisation' the world comes up with the verdict will always be that there is a need for redemption. Ironically the world too is faithful to its character! Indeed it is the world which will, in part, determine how the church improvises for the church must relate to the world. If the church does not relate to the world she is no longer being faithful to her call. The world will always improvise according to its nature and the church's improvisation must be in part related to how the world is acting at a specific time.[20] So it is most appropriate that the call is given to the church to improvise in a way that is faithful to the story line.

Thus on the three main areas of difference I consider that the real difference is minimal and that the analogy remains as a most suitable one to apply to Scripture.[21]

End of Excursus

3.   Equal to serve

Before approaching the key restrictive texts I want to indicate that, in the light of the above approach to Scripture and the hermeneutical principles suggested earlier, that the New Testament overwhelmingly supports a place for women within the Christian community that gives them equal opportunity alongside men to serve.

Gretchen Gaebelein Hull in her book Equal to Serve, says 'Secular feminism centres around gaining equal rights; biblical feminism

---

[20]Surely the contrast we discover between Romans 13 and Revelation 13 (where both passages deal with the required relationship of the church to the state) gives us an illustration of the church's required 'improvisation' in response to the actions of the world.

[21]In using the analogy I, of course, acknowledge that I begin with a model of Scripture which this analogy helps explain. For someone who begins with another model of Scripture the analogy would fall down, not because Scripture and a play cannot be compared, but that the Scriptures, in their mind, serve another purpose to the one I have outlined. The model I am working with will be scary to some, particularly those who wish to talk of the sufficiency of Scripture, but my challenge to them is to define what they mean by this term, for the Bible *as text* is insufficient on certain matters, but as story will demand a great level of humility and prove to be totally sufficient. Improvisation does not mean that I can put something together that suits my own ends with no reference to what has gone before, but neither can I simply stay within the text of Scripture. My point being that we might have to go beyond the text of Scripture but cannot become divorced from the story of Scripture.

centres around equal opportunity to serve.'[22] Under the new covenant, it is not the outward shell that is important but the life within. Paul says the outward shell is wasting away (2 Corinthians 4:16) but the life within is eternal (4:18). It is the life source within which is important — this life source is none other than the promised Holy Spirit who is poured out on all flesh, irrespective of gender. The outward shell must extend to cover the issue of gender, for to see people restricted because of their gender is surely to take a worldly viewpoint.

As a result of the Fall, men and women became adversaries, competitors and even oppressors — instead of co-operators and joint administrators of our inheritance. In Christ this harmony is restored to us. Male and female can again jointly administrate the original commission God gave of bringing his rule to bear on the earth. In offering the same renewal and salvation to all — regardless of race, gender or class – He gives the same high calling, responsibility and privilege to all. Both male and female are equal ambassadors for Christ and his gospel (2 Corinthians 5:14-21), for both males and females are being transformed into the image of Christ (2 Corinthians 3:18, cf. Genesis 1:26-28).

If this is truly the situation that the gospel proclaims we should be provoked to ask why then does Paul, in particular, seem to restrict women. In other words we begin with the transforming power of the gospel, and see the restrictive passages as exceptions rather than as the rule. To these we now will direct our attention.

---

[22](London: Scripture Union, 1987), p. 56.

CHAPTER 6

RESTRICTIVE PASSAGES

There are three main Scriptural passages which have been understood to restrict the role and function of women within the church. They are, in canonical order, 1 Corinthians 11:2-16; 14:34f.; and 1 Timothy 2:11-15. The first one concerns certain customs that Paul desired to be in place, the second addresses an issue of disorderly speaking and the third instructs Timothy to bring necessary correction to a situation in Ephesus. I will seek in this chapter to give an explanation for these three Scriptures, which I trust will be true exegetically, and will indicate that these instructions are not to be applied universally to women in all situations. I leave the reader to decide how successful I am in the process. However, even if I am found to be unconvincing, I am suggesting that given the contingent nature of Paul's letters, none of these texts can, by themselves, be automatically used to bring about a universal restriction on women.[1]

I am aware that I am close to saying 'if you don't agree with my exegesis I still can't be wrong because I can simply eliminate the texts through consigning them to the bin of contingency'. I trust that I am a little more honest than that — I am suggesting that there are good exegetical grounds for reading the texts in a non-restrictive way, but

---

[1]By contingent it is meant that they were written to a specific *situation* at a specific *time* to deal with specific *issues*. Obviously by so stating this does not secure the position that these instructions are not universally applicable. Many contingent instructions are universally applicable. 'Let the thief no longer steal' might have been stated for contingent reasons, but is universally applicable. The three main passages we will look at are correcting abusive practice — to make those automatically applicable would mean that we would have to make sure we have understood the practice being corrected, that our situation was the same as (or significantly similar to) the one being corrected, and that the applied correction was in line with overarching theological perspectives.

even if these particular Scriptures were found to be restrictive (from an exegetical perspective), that hermeneutically we would still need to ask whether for theological grounds they are universally applicable. Again presuppositions will determine conclusions to a large extent. If our presupposition is that Paul believed in the hierarchy of men over women and that only men should hold governmental positions then these texts could be evidence for us confirming that position; if, however, the presupposition is that men and women have an equal right to serve in leadership and that we believe that this was Paul's viewpoint, then we will wish to see these texts as correcting a situation at a specific time and being capable of being explained in such a way that does not contradict our presupposition.

1.   The Corinthian situation

The church at Corinth was founded by Paul around 50AD, with the first letter being written some three or four years later. It is evident that a major error had crept into the church: the error of over-realized eschatology. In simple terms this meant that the Corinthians understood their current experience of the Spirit as evidence that the end had already come, thus effectively denying that the end was still a future event. (The New Testament picture is one where the kingdom of God has 'already' come, but 'not yet' in its fullness; the Corinthians had so exaggerated the 'already' that there was no fullness yet to come.)

For the Corinthians, the Spirit belongs to the eschaton (the end), and they believed they were already experiencing the Spirit in full measure. Some of them made exaggerated claims (see Paul's somewhat sarcastic comments: 'Already you have all you want! Already you have become rich! Quite apart from us you have become kings! Indeed, I wish that you had become kings, so that we might be kings with you!' (1 Corinthians 4:8)), and it is perhaps they who understood tongues as the language of angels (1 Corinthians 13:1), this being a further indication to them that they had already arrived as they were already speaking the language of heaven. This exaggerated viewpoint led them to believe they were living a spiritual existence above the physical existence of this present age.[2] One extreme result for some was the loss of a belief in a future bodily resurrection (addressed by Paul in chapter 15), while with some of the women this error seems to have manifested itself with sexless marriages (addressed in the opening verses of chapter 7).

If this analysis of over-realized eschatology is the major factor that I suggest, we can easily understand that the Corinthian church was experiencing many difficulties. And if marriage itself was being undermined by 'spiritual' women, we would expect that the relationship between men and women within the wider community was in confusion. These 'spiritual' women were beyond marriage, indeed beyond any of the restraints of this age. This background and the impact of this error on marriage needs to be borne in mind when approaching the two passages we will examine.

1.1 Women to cover their heads: 1 Corinthians 11:2-16

This passage is the most difficult exegetically, but is perhaps the easiest to deal with in respect of women and their roles. In fact it can be argued that far from restricting women, it encourages them to function equally (at least in public prayer and prophecy) alongside men; for Paul nowhere places a restriction on them in these verses, he merely adjusts *how* they were praying and prophesying.

1.1.1 A passage of commendation

Before seeking to exegete the passage we need to stand back somewhat from the details and examine the overall thrust. He begins in verse 2 by commending them for holding on to the traditions he had passed on to them. (This is in direct contrast to his words in verse 17 relating to the Lord's Supper where he cannot find anything to commend

---

[2]See Fee, *1 Corinthians*, NICNT commentary (Grand Rapids: Eerdmans, 1987), pp. 12f. Likewise G. J. Laughery's article, 'Paul: Anti-marriage? Anti-sex? Ascetic? A dialogue with 1 Corinthians 7:1-40', *Evangelical Quarterly*, Vol. LXIX. No. 2 (April, 1997), pp. 109-128, looks at the over-realized background to 1 Corinthians.

in their practice at all. Their practice of the Lord's Supper was a denial of the unity and fellowship it was intended to demonstrate, and to such an extent that it perpetuated the fallen division caused by economic disparity.) Having commended them in verse 2, Paul then seeks to bring a correction through the words 'now I want you to realise'. This indicates that we need to decide what he is commending them for and what he is bringing correction to. There are two practices going on in this passage: the men and the women are praying, and there is a problem with headcovering. He corrects the latter, so he cannot be commending them for their practice. This then leaves us with only one option for his commendation: they had been allowing men and women to function equally alongside one another in the public assembly, which in the light of the gospel would have been the appropriate response to the tradition deposited by Paul. His commendation in verse 2 is for the equality that they are demonstrating, while his condemnation in verse 17 is for the inequality that they are perpetuating. Hence in taking a step back from the passage we discover that, far from encountering a set of verses that bring restriction to women's function, these verses actually endorse a woman functioning equally alongside a man — although they do bring a corrective to how they functioned.

1.1.2 Some key decisions

This passage raises a number of key questions, some of which we will be unable to answer conclusively. We find Paul using the word 'head' which raises two questions: does he use this in two different ways, one anatomical and the other metaphorical? Also what is the meaning he attaches to the word when he uses it metaphorically? What custom is being addressed: is it headcovering? If so, is it the men or the women who are in error? What precisely does he mean by the word 'glory' which is in some way tied to his appeal to creation? There are other issues that will need to be addressed as the passage is exegeted, but I suggest it will be more helpful to come to some conclusions on the particular issues highlighted prior to the exegesis of the passage. These I will now seek to address.

- How does Paul use the word 'head'?

There are clearly anatomical references to a man or a woman's 'head' throughout these verses, such as the references to men praying with their heads covered being a dishonouring thing to do (11:4). However, the second reference to head can be taken either anatomically and by natural extension to be a reference to himself (i.e. he dishonours himself), or as a reference back to his head being Christ (11:3). This is not an easy call to make and could be understood as a reference to both, that is, a man praying in such a way dishonours both himself and Christ. Given the ambiguity of Paul's usage here I suggest that we should not close the options down but understand it as a primary reference to Christ but also secondarily as a reference to the man (and men in general).

Of greater debate is the conflict among scholars on the meaning of the word 'head' (Greek: *kephale*) during this period. Simplifying the issues enormously the choice is between head with connotations of authority and position (similar to our head of a company), or head meaning 'source' (such as the head of a river is its source). The matter is not easy to settle and I like the comments of Gretchen Hull's words that 'The Apostles themselves describe the role of the head in such a way that *in practice* it makes no difference whether head represents an empowered figure or a source figure.'[3] When we come to exegete the

---

[3]Gretchen Gaebelein Hull, *Equal to Serve* (London: Scripture Union, 1989) p. 205, italics original. I had originally intended to include an appendix on the discussion regarding the meaning of the word 'head', but decided that the jury is still out on this issue. I was leaning towards a meaning that was closer to the first suggestion but obviously strongly modified so that the type of authority envisaged was in line with the discussions in chapter 1 on authority. I am now more open to the possibility that the meaning in this passage is 'source', particularly as Paul goes on to say that the source of the woman's existence was the man, who he also

passage we will have to decide what are the implications of Paul's use of 'head' even if we are unable to determine its meaning.

- What custom is being addressed?

There are three viable possibilities: 1) that the women should have their heads covered; 2) that the men should not be covering their heads; or 3) that this is not a reference to headcovering at all, but to the inappropriate way in which the women were wearing their hair.

This last proposal has been argued by James Hurley (and others) in various places.[4] He suggests that women were violating the accepted custom of wearing one's hair up. These women were loosing their hair, thus effectively showing off their faddish hairstyles which was inappropriate in a worship context. Suffice it to say that Fee's critique has shown Hurley's position to be problematic. The appropriate position advocated for the women (hair up) must equally apply in the opposite direction for the men (hair down). So Fee notes that if a woman's head being 'uncovered' simply means that she has 'her hair let down', how can 'the man's not covering his head in v. 7 [be] the opposite of this.'[5] Further if we take, as Hurley does, that verse 15 suggests that long hair

---

describes as her head. I suggest that an article such as 'Head' in the *Dictionary of Paul and his letters*, could be a good starting point as some important articles are cited there.

[4]For example in *Man and Woman in Biblical Perspective* (London: IVP, 1981). See Fee, *1 Corinthians*, p. 496 for references to other writers with this viewpoint. I have grossly simplified Hurley's suggestion. He also makes an appeal to the words that Paul uses, which are not the normal words for veiling, but 'down from the head' which he suggests better fit a description of the hair hanging down. Hurley says that the only specific reference to a veil is in v. 15 where Paul says that hair is given to a woman instead of (*anti*) a veil, and that the churches have no such custom as veiling (v. 16).

[5]Fee, ibid., p. 496. Fee does acknowledge whatever solution is suggested that none of them are without their difficulties. He concludes with a comment that 'a modified form of the traditional view seems to have fewer difficulties' (p. 497) and goes on to describe this view as holding that the covering in view is a loose shawl, not a veil.

is given *instead* of a covering (literally a 'wrap around') this would actually imply the necessity of the women having their hair in some way down — the very opposite of what Hurley has been saying is appropriate in these preceding verses. Keener concludes with, 'It is thus clear that head coverings, not merely long hair, are in view.'[6]

The second proposal suggests that the issue being addressed is that of headcovering, but rather than the problem being that of women uncovering their heads, it is the Corinthian men who were covering theirs. This proposal is argued for by Neil Elliott in his book, *Liberating Paul.*[7] He contends that when commentators have applied these verses to women and their need to cover their heads that the 'argument of these verses has proven almost impenetrable on that assumption.' Calling on historical evidence that a Roman man would normally cover his head when coming before the gods of the city, often through pulling his toga over his head. For a Christian man to do this in worship would be to adopt 'a gesture recognized throughout the empire as the sign of *pietas*, and thus to emulate the emperor's own virtue.' Such behaviour 'would dishonour the man's head, since that head is Christ — the one whom Caesar's subordinate in Judea had crucified.'[8] If then it was the social elite who were adopting this custom, they would have been drawing attention to their status in society. The strength of this proposal is that Paul begins in verse 3 with establishing that the head of every *man* is Christ, and follows it up in the next verse with 'every *man* who prays or prophecies with his head covered dishonours his head'. So, although there is more material in the passage addressed to the women, Paul actually begins by addressing the men not the women, thus indicating that it is the men that he will seek to correct.

---

[6]*Paul*, p.22.
[7](New York: Orbis, 1994; Sheffield: Sheffield Academic Press, 1995), pp. 209-211. See p. 205, n. 107 for references to other supporting scholars.
[8]Ibid., p.210.

This proposal is attractive and brings these verses into line with Paul's directives on the Lord's Supper. In those verses (11:17-22) Paul criticises those who were abusing the Lord's Supper and allowing it to become another means by which social and economic divisions were perpetuated. Elliott's proposal therefore makes the verses we are discussing (11:2-16) also verses that Paul corrects those who were perpetuating their superior social status. However, rather than being a factor that strengthens Elliott's argument, this is actually, in my opinion, its weakness. It is Paul himself who indicates that his directives on headcovering and the Lord's Supper are very different. On the former he states that he can commend them, while on the latter he cannot commend them (11:2 contrasted with 11:17). If the practice surrounding the Lord's Supper brought about Paul's condemnation because the Corinthians were perpetuating division and inequality, it seems likely, as already discussed, that he commends them in these earlier verses precisely for maintaining an equality. Thus it is more likely that we have women seeking to act on a par with the men, than socially elite men who through their act of headcovering were underlining their superiority.

Again, the argument that Elliott uses, that Paul begins with references to the men in verses 3 and 4, do not need to be taken as an indication that it is the men that he is correcting. As we will see it is more likely he begins with a reference to men first to balance out his correction of the women.

I suggest, then, that the argument that Paul is correcting the men fails to convincingly deliver. Therefore, I come down on the side of the first proposal above: that Paul is actually addressing a situation where women were uncovering their heads in worship. Fee argues that as Paul progresses his argument that, 'in each instance the argument seems aimed specifically at the women'.[9]

---

[9] *1 Corinthians*, p. 495.

I will seek through the exegesis of the passage to indicate that it is the issue of the women who were uncovering their heads that best fits with Paul's argument. It should be sufficient to note that Keener has amassed considerable evidence for the practice of headcovering for women in the Ancient Mediterranean setting.[10] I will simply draw from his research to indicate that a woman's hair revealed her beauty and was a potential factor in provoking a man's lust within Greek and Jewish tradition. I quote two paragraphs from Keener:

> Loosening a woman's hair could reveal her beauty and subject her to male lust in both Greek and Jewish tradition. Early Roman women were divorced for not wearing veils precisely because their action laid them open to the suspicion that they were looking for another man.
>
> A Jewish woman who ventured into public with her hair down and exposed to view, or who otherwise could be accused of flirtatious behavior, could be divorced with no financial support from her marriage contract. A woman uncovering her head could be described as nearing the final stage in seducing a man. Jewish teachers permitted loosing a woman's hair only in the case of an adulterous woman, who was publicly shamed by exposure to the sight of men; but even then they warned that it should not be done with women whose hair was extremely beautiful, lest the young priests be moved to lust.[11]

There is considerable evidence that for women to uncover their heads would have been sexually provocative and therefore inappropriate behaviour. Coupled with class conflict at Corinth (as indicated in the divisions at the Lord's Supper), there might have been a tendency for some of the women from a higher class background to feel freer to uncover their heads, showing off their fashionable hairstyles and

---

[10]*Paul*, pp. 22-23.
[11]Ibid., p. 29.

jewellery. If this is so, then those from a more humble class background could have understood those who uncovered their heads as being wilfully seductive.[12]

There might be a class issue involved here, but I suggest that the overriding issue again is that of an over-realized eschatology. I suspect that the scenario in Corinth is fairly simple to understand. Paul's teaching was that of equality of function which the Corinthian church had held on to (11:2). This teaching naturally raised a question for the women: if they were equal to the men why did they have to continue to cover their heads? Equality surely meant that they could pray and prophesy as the men did — with their heads uncovered. Sexual differences and (for some) sexual activity was something that only belonged to this age. They were living in the eschatological age, so anything that continued to emphasise this present age had to be removed. Hence their response to the gospel was both appropriate and inappropriate. As far as belonging to the new humanity, they were right to affirm the equality of function, but they were wrong to deny the continuing differences between the genders. The behaviour of the women in uncovering their heads would only lead to the problems of lust and immorality being multiplied. A modern day Western equivalent (and by giving this I do not intend to be in any way crude, but only to indicate the severity of the situation) might be that of women praying and prophesying scantily dressed or even topless. Far from being a sign that endorsed equality, it would be something that would need major correction. Appropriate dress was an issue then, and continues to be so.

- Glory

In verse 7, Paul uses the word *doxa* ('glory') twice, once that man is the (image and) glory of God while the woman is the glory of man. Fee admits that trying to define the term *doxa* in this context is like trying to

---

[12]See Keener, ibid., pp. 30f.

pick up mercury between one's fingers![13] He suggests that Paul probably intends it to mean that a person is to bring honour and praise to the one who is their head. This implies that a man who acts in an inappropriate way (praying or prophesying with his head covered) does not set God in the right place, and likewise when a woman acts inappropriately (praying or prophesying with her head uncovered) does not set a man (and specifically her husband) in the right place. The opposite of the term 'glory', as used in this passage, would then be 'dishonour' (11:4f.).

Paul's words in verse 7, 'For a man ought not to have his head veiled, since he is the image and reflection of God; but woman is the reflection of man', can be read as extremely hierarchical, although it is vital that we do not misread Paul and assume he is denying that women are also in the image of God. It is important to note that Paul does not intend to deny that a woman brings glory to God when behaving appropriately; he simply does not expand his discussion to include this aspect here as he is being singular and focused. For a woman to pray or prophesy uncovered would not honour a man, whereas if she prayed or prophesied covered this would honour her head and bring glory to him. He focuses on this one aspect as the Corinthian problem was the wrong expression of relationships between men and women, and specifically between husbands and wives. The women were bringing dishonour to their husbands, by appearing seductive, so Paul strongly puts them in their place and calls them to honour their husbands, without ever restricting their spiritual equality.

---

[13]Fee, *1 Corinthians*, pp. 515f.

1.1.3 Brief exegesis of 11:2-16[14]

Verse 2. The Corinthians had held on to equality between the genders and Paul commends them for this.

Verse 3. Having praised them he also needs to correct their practice, and makes an appeal to headship in order to do this. He does not give a logical progression of God — man — woman, which would indicate a strict hierarchical view, but gives three examples of headship. His point is that headship exists and must have an impact on our relationships.[15] So he begins with the statement that every male (or husband) has Christ as their head. If Christ is their head they must be motivated to place him in the right place. If anything is done which does not place Christ in that appointed place, then they have sinned by dishonouring their head.

Having established that Christ is the head of every male (without necessarily denying, in this context, that the head of every woman could also be described as Christ),[16] he passes on to the marriage relationship

---

[14]The commentary by Fee is generally reckoned to be one of the finest NT commentaries available, and I suggest that those who wish a detailed exegesis read his comments. I will restrict the exegesis here as the key decisions have already been made in the preceding comments.

[15]Perhaps a meaning that in some ways straddles the authority / source argument could be one indicating dependency. This would indicate that just as Christ cannot act independently of the Godhead, so neither men and women can act independently of each other. Taking this perspective would not necessarily indicate a hierarchical perspective (particularly given that later in this same passage Paul stresses mutual inter-dependence).

[16]In Ephesians we have two applications of headship: Christ and the church, and the husband in relationship to his wife. He picks up on the headship within marriage in this passage here, and the headship of Christ in relationship to every male could be a shorthand way of expressing Christ's headship to the church. This would understand Paul to be meaning something like: Christ is head of the church, so head of all those who have been redeemed, and this headship must shape up the marriage relationship, therefore we can practically speak of his headship being to every redeemed male. However, it is possible that Paul intends us to understand this headship in the Corinthian passage to carry some cosmic dimension such as Christ being the firstborn of the new creation: again this would

where the husband is the head of the wife. He is able therefore to call for the wife to relate to her husband in a way that will not dishonour him. Although this passage can be addressed to men and women in general, the headship argument, I believe, is limited to husbands and wives. I maintain this as Paul does not say that the head of every woman is man but that the head of *a* woman is *the* man; and also as the culture of the day meant that women were generally married and writers were not sensitive in their instructions to include all exceptions.

Next he states that Christ's head was God. Christ did not come to fulfil his own desires, and although equal with God submitted to the will of the Father. His fulfilment was not in independence, but in yielding to the Father's will. So Paul's desire is not to indicate a hierarchy, but to establish headship as a principle, and that where it is in place, all parties need to honour those relationships by living in an appropriate way. The headship relationship that will have an impact on appropriate male and female behaviour is placed in the middle, between two key statements. The first establishes that men / husbands do not have a freedom to do whatever they want, and there are no exceptions as it applies to *every* man. Later Paul will bring a restriction over how the women prayed and prophesied, but he establishes first that men must be in line. The final example is that of Christ's yielding to the will of the Father whose behaviour is the example for all believers to follow. (I suggest that had Paul been dealing with men as the problem here in Corinth he might well have taken another approach all together — he shapes his arguments to the situation.)

Verses 4-6. Although he does not defend his statements with sustained reasoning, he maintains that dishonour would be the result of men praying or prophesying with their heads covered. They would dishonour their head which is probably a reference to Christ, although by

---

not be a headship that excludes wives. Paul focuses on husbands for this suits his purpose here. He is simply pressing for one outcome: good horizontal marriage relationships and is not drawn beyond this purpose.

implication it could be a reference to their own (physical) head (and by extension to mean their own gender).

The opposite would be true for women, and the dishonour is to such an extent that he suggests even if they were to have their heads shaved they could not act any more dishonouringly. This could mean that Paul is provoking them to take their actions to a logical conclusion. If by having their heads uncovered is to act in a mannish way why should they stop there? Why not go further and have mannish hair? He knows that they would object to this (see verses 6, 14f.), but he says both are mannish so either both are appropriate or both are inappropriate. They cannot argue for the inappropriateness of one and the appropriateness of the other.[17]

The other possibility is that we might have here a reference to cult prostitutes who some think might have shaved their heads. If this is so then Paul is arguing that to act in a way that dishonours the marriage (appearing seductive) is all but as bad as acting as a prostitute. However, as Evans says in response to this suggestion, 'We cannot be completely sure of what the customs were.'[18] So more probably Paul is suggesting that they might as well go the whole way and make themselves bald.

Verses 7-10. These verses contain appeals to creation. It needs to be remembered that Paul appeals to creation not to silence the women, but to insist on their need to cover their heads; so it is important that we do not read into these verses more than is being said. In verse 7 the male is the image of God, which immediately indicates that Paul is thinking of the creation narrative. He drops the term 'image' when referring to the women for they are not the 'image of man' thus making it clear that he is arguing for women in their right relationship with their husbands, not for some hierarchy before God. Women are to bring honour to their

---

[17]This is Fee's argument, *1 Corinthians*, p. 512.
[18]Evans, *Woman*, p. 88.

husbands, and by dressing seductively they were not doing this at all. Again we remember that he is correcting the women so his words can appear very strong. Appealing to creation he reminds them that the woman was created *from* and *for* the man (verses 8f.). The women at Corinth were acting in independence, but Paul's appeal to creation gives women a role only in relation to men / husbands. (I again underline the nature of Paul's argument. It is for a purpose: to deal with women who are out of line specifically in relation to their own husbands. He is not endorsing a male supremacy for they are subject to Christ and his example. If the men had been out of line in Corinth I suspect that Paul would have been arguing very differently. He is strong, but if we do not read more into it than he intends, or if we do not remove it from the corrective context, we will also see that it is sensitively written.)

Verse 10. is not an easy one to understand. I suggest that it is best understood as bringing this appeal from creation to a close. (He begins with, 'For this reason...', indicating that creation suggests the rightness of the woman having authority on her head. Most translations add words such as 'a sign of' to make sense of the Greek, which literally reads, 'For this reason a woman ought to *have authority over her head*, because of the angels.') My proposal is that we understand this verse in the light of what has preceded, with the argument advancing as follows: creation indicates that the woman should not act independently and so it is only appropriate that she accepts her womanhood and role within marriage, and does not appear seductive. She therefore needs to be covered not as an argument that she can only do what her husband allows, but rather as an acknowledgement that there are certain (cultural) modes of dress that are inappropriate for a married woman.

It is possible, though, that Paul is not pressing the argument from creation to a conclusion but is now presenting another perspective altogether by affirming that the woman has the right to choose over the issue of headcovering (if we understand Paul meaning that the woman has authority *over* her own head). If this is the right understanding of this verse we would still come to a similar practical conclusion as Paul implies that she should forgo this right. This seems to me to be unlikely as the language of verse 10 seems to imply a continuation of the arguments thus far, and it is with verse 11 that there is a shift with the word 'nevertheless'.

So I suggest that Paul is continuing to refer to the need for headcovering (understanding the word 'authority' to be an unusual shorthand way of saying, 'a sign that she has authority'); verse 10 then being be a continuation of the creation argument, with the woman needing to accept her place of submission within marriage and indicating this through her headcovering.[19] Whichever way it is understood there is the need for compliance with what is fitting and honouring.

Also in line with his appeal to creation, Paul gives a reference to the presence of angels. This reference could be due to his belief that the angels themselves might be tempted sexually (as per the Jewish understanding of Genesis 6), but it is more likely a simple illustration that angels are respectors of the created order and the women should also be. (Another viable possibility could be that given Paul's earlier reference to the judging of angels by the saints (1 Corinthians 6:3), he is referring to angels here to indicate that: if they will make such judgements, one day surely they are capable of making responsible choices now over the issue of headcovering.)

Verses 11,12. Paul begins with a new line of argument here and by doing so corrects any misunderstanding that might have taken place already. He has come close to arguing for an inferior position for women (created *from* and *for* man), and has felt obliged to argue strongly in order to bring these women back in line, but he now ensures that his

---

[19]For detailed discussions of these points see Keener, *Paul*, pp. 39-42; Fee, *1 Corinthians*, pp. 518-522. They both argue for the plain meaning being that of a woman having authority over her head, i.e. Paul affirms that she has the right to choose.

argument cannot be taken beyond what he intended to establish. Indeed it is in these verses we discover what Paul would like to see established, namely that of the mutual interdependence of men and women. This is the way it is 'in the Lord', and even the natural process of giving birth indicates that God intends mutuality. Eve might owe her existence to Adam, but since that first creation, every man has come into the world though women, and both men and women are 'from God'.

Verses 13-16. In the opening verses he did not invite any assessment: he told them how things were, hitting very hard at the women who were acting out of line. He then ensured that they had not taken his strength of argument beyond his desired position which he outlined in verses 11 and 12. The tone of his argument softens again significantly from this point on. He now appeals to them to judge the issue for themselves. Although there are cultural values referred to here by Paul ('nature' is the Greek word *phusis* which can carry the connotation of 'culture' and probably does here), his bottom line appeal is that the woman's hair is her glory, it brings her honour. It seems that Paul is arguing along the line of, 'if nature has given her a covering then it is only right that this is endorsed by the wearing of a covering'. His final appeal then is to quote the practices of the other churches: they are all continuing to live within the appropriate custom.

1.1.4 Conclusion on 1 Corinthians 11:2-16

This passage, although not an easy one to exegete, is aimed to correct a disorder. The disorder was that of women, who in the light of their (right) belief in equality were (wrongly) seeking to express that unity in a way that was dishonouring to their own husbands and bringing shame[20]

---

[20]The term 'shame' appears in both the 'restrictive' passages in Corinthians. The culture of the day was that of honour-shame which reinforced the social conventions, so the references to shame could be an appeal to cultural appropriateness, so in this passage in question Paul's appeal would be that for women to be uncovered was to commit an act that (culturally) shamed their husbands, and thus an offence to the gospel.

on their own gender. Paul initially argues very strongly to ensure that the women understood that creation itself indicated that they were to be in relation to the men, but quickly ensures that no-one pushes this further than mutual-dependence. Finally he appeals to their own sense of what is right. The argument becomes softer as the text progresses and Keener warns that we should not compare the progression of Paul's logic with one that we would be comfortable with. He even suggests that 'In ancient debate, one might give arguments for a position that were different from the reasons one held to the position itself. Paul has to address the issue of women's head coverings in Corinth with the arguments that would most readily persuade his ancient readers.' And in the light of that comment Keener says, 'Had he [Paul] been writing a letter to us he would have dealt with entirely different issues and reasoned a different way. It is easy for modern Western readers to assume that cultures elsewhere think as we do; we are impatient with other cultures' logic.'[21]

Whether I have successfully understood Paul's line of arguing or not, we are left with a passage that commends the Corinthians for maintaining equality of function among the congregation regardless of gender. Thus the passage, although difficult exegetically, is not a difficult passage in the sense of being restrictive to women.

Through examining this passage I cannot prove that Paul insisted on total equality of function, nor that he did not hold to a hierarchical view of marriage. On the other hand, I suggest that the most that could be made of this passage by those who take an opposite viewpoint to myself would be that Paul thought that the husband as head of his wife, being rooted in a creation order, gave him a place of authority — however, that authority should be exercised in a Christlike fashion — and that although he allowed for equality of function publicly that this did not extend to the situation of governmental authority. The passage by itself

---

[21]Keener, *Paul*, p. 31.

then does not yield to either side in clear language exactly what we would like it to say, but at least we can insist that we have no basis in this passage on which to restrict women exercising public ministry alongside men.

1.2 Women to be silent: 1 Corinthians 14:34-35

There are serious questions over whether these verses were ever originally penned by Paul. Gordon Fee takes the line that they were 'not part of the original text, but were a very early gloss that was subsequently placed in the text at two different places.'[22] Likewise, and from a less conservative stance, Neil Elliott states that these verses 'are interpolations into Paul's genuine letter, made after the apostle's death.'[23]

However, if we accept these verses as canonical, whether by Paul's hand or not, is there a means by which they can be read which is not universally restrictive, but solely applicable to the situation at Corinth? I suggest that this is indeed possible.[24]

The context of Paul's instructions on the charismata (spiritual gifts) is that of bringing order and discipline, for 'everything should be done in a fitting and orderly way' (14:40), and within the chapter he has given specific instructions with regard to two disorderly situations, both of which relate to disorderly speech. In the first incident he brings

---

[22]Fee, *1 Corinthians*, p. 699. The text is found in some manuscripts following v. 33, and in others following v. 40. It is suggested that they were added to combat a rising feminist movement at the end of the first or at the beginning of the second century.

[23]*Liberating Paul* (Sheffield: Sheffield Academic Press, 1995), p. 25.

[24]The solution that I suggest in the ensuing paragraphs of the main text is the one that I prefer, but I include one other possibility here. It has been suggested that the restriction on women is not from Paul, but is a quote from Judaisers that Paul now responds to. He then disagrees totally with the quote in vv. 36-38. This solution would also enable the phrase 'as the law says' to be a reference to the Jewish oral law.

adjustment to disorderly tongues speaking, and in the second it is prophets and their practice that he corrects. In these verses which we want to examine, there is a correction to women who are involved in disorderly speech.

There is a close link between the three situations, for in each case we find that there is a problem with disorderly speech, this is followed by a prohibition which is given in each occasion using the same Greek word, *sigao* (to be silent), and finally there is an alternative suggested by Paul. So we find that he instructs tongues speakers to be silent if there is no interpreter present (14:27f.). Tongues, spoken publicly without an interpretation is disorderly (the problem), therefore under such a situation the tongues speaker is instructed to keep quiet (*sigao*) and to speak to him/herself and to God (the alternative). In 14:29-32 Paul, likewise addresses the prophet that prophesies in such a way that others cannot contribute (the problem). That prophet is to stop (*sigao*) and let another speak so as all can be instructed (the alternative). In both those cases the speaking itself is not wrong, but the manner in which the speaking is being carried out is causing disorder and confusion. The same type of correction is then applied to the situation in Corinth with certain women whose speaking must be silenced (*sigao*). If we read between the lines we discover that the problem in Corinth is that some women were asking questions in such a way that disorder resulted (the problem), and so Paul tells them to be silent. The alternative he gives is for them to ask their husbands at home, for he wants them to learn.

The situation being addressed is no different to a disorderly classroom where a teacher might well say to one of the pupils, 'Be quiet (*sigao*), you are not allowed to talk in class.' If later the teacher were to ask the same child to answer a question, we would be very surprised if the pupil refused on the basis of the teacher's rebuke that was meant to cover a specific situation of disorderly speech.

Now let us take a closer look at these verses. In the light of the fact that verses 34 and 35 appear in different places in the manuscripts it is best to take these two verses as a unit, in other words to place the phrase 'as in all the congregation of the saints' with the previous paragraph (unlike the NIV), and to begin a paragraph with the opening words of verse 34, 'Women should remain silent in the churches.'

Verse 34. We have noted that the term 'remain silent' is not only the same Greek word used earlier, but we can now add that it is also in the same command 'mood'. This should indicate to us that we should interpret it in similar fashion to the prohibition aimed at the disorderly tongues speakers and prophets. It should not be taken as an absolute prohibition, but a correction of disorder. These women are not allowed to speak (Greek: *lalein*). The word used here is not one that relates to 'official' speaking in a church context — it is not a prohibition against preaching or teaching (Greek: *kerussein* or *didaskein*). Rather, the word used is a straightforward one that refers to the simple act of speaking — the context must indicate what is meant. It would appear that the alternative outlet for this 'speaking' is for the women to ask their questions in another setting, so one can make the fairly safe assumption that the prohibition is aimed at stopping the asking of questions in a wrong setting.

Women are to be in submission as the law indicates. It seems best to understand the sense here as being of a submission to the assembled church, rather than to their husbands.[25] The phrase 'as the law says' does not fit well if the text is genuinely Pauline, as he only uses this phrase of the written law, but the written law does not state a

---

[25] See Fee, *1 Corinthians*, p. 707. He comments, 'What is not clear is whether the women are to be subject to their own husbands or to the church as a whole in its worship. More likely it is the latter.'

specific submission of women.[26] I suggest that the only way we can take it is as a general appeal to the law as endorsing order, thus understanding Paul to mean that the law speaks of order and women need to submit to that order.

Verse 35. The women had been asking questions in a disorderly way. Paul is keen not to dissuade the women from asking questions, but he wishes to redirect their questions. He does this by suggesting that they address them outside of the church gatherings to their own husbands at home. He closes with the further statement that the speaking (Greek: *lalein*) within the church is a disgrace.

The issue of women speaking out of turn can be illustrated from two more modern situations. Leroy Birney originally published a paper in 1971 called 'The role of women in the New Testament church' and added a postscript to it in 1979. In the postscript he writes, 'For example, I would no longer reject out-of-hand the possibility that the problem was women shouting across the aisle to ask their husbands questions since I have seen similar interruptions in new churches in Colombia.'[27]

Another example is to be found in the experience of James McKeown in his work in Ghana. Within that culture (where the women were seen very much as second class) he discovered that if the women were not told that they had to come to a meeting to learn, then they would simply gossip and chatter among themselves.'[28]

So it is likely that some of the women in Corinth were chattering or asking questions in a vocal and disturbing way within the assembled church. This might be because they were, as in the examples above,

[26]See Fee, ibid., where he notes that the oral law (the teachings of the Jewish rabbis) did tell women to be submissive. Paul never refers to the oral law as 'the law', so it is unlikely that this is a reference to it here.
[27]*Christian Brethren Review Journal*, No. 33, pp. 15-32; quote on p. 30.
[28]Christine Leonard, *A Giant in Ghana* (Chichester: New Wine, 1989), p. 109.

somewhat uneducated and viewed as second class. Keener suggests that as women were generally less educated than the men, the problem that was arising in Corinth was that the women were setting the pace for learning through their constant questions for clarification. Paul then advises the women to receive private attention and education in order that they might catch up to the basics of Christian instruction that the rest of the congregation knows. Thus the 'short-range solution was that the women were to stop interrupting the service; the long-range solution was that they were to learn the knowledge they had been lacking.'[29]

This is certainly a most plausible solution, but it might also be noted that with the underlying error of over-realized eschatology in the Corinthian church, that there could well have been a number of women who were disrespectful to the assembled people in making comments in such a way that they were not being in submission. They considered that they were exhibiting their freedom and spirituality, but the result was chaos and the absence of order.

This latter suggestion would explain why there is such a strong instruction for the women to ask their own husbands in the home situation. This could be understood as a major put down of the women (and might indeed be so if the text is not genuine). If, however, we assume the text is authentically Pauline, we could see a pastoral corrective in the suggested solution. Paul's instruction not only allows the women to ask their questions, but he hits very hard in order to direct them back into their own marriage relationship which, they being spiritual, had now outgrown.[30]

---

[29] *Paul*, pp. 83,88.

[30] This solution does not cover single women, nor would it have been appropriate for women whose husbands were not believers. However the writers of the time were not as sensitive toward the issue of including all parties and the expectation would have been for those situations that fell outside of the ruling given to be resolved in another suitable way.

Whether the solution is the simple one of uneducated women asking their questions, or it relates to over-spiritual women causing a disturbance through exercising a false spirituality (or indeed it is a combination of the two), we can safely conclude that we do not find here a universal prohibition of women taking part in ministry in the church (indeed if this were the case we would have a reversal of the situation that Paul endorsed only a few chapters earlier).

2. Women not to teach: 1 Timothy 2:11-15

2.1 The background to the letter: false teachers

This passage of Scripture can seem to be the most negative toward women. It is the only one that explicitly prohibits women from teaching, and there are direct appeals to creation which could appear to endorse a rigid hierarchy.

Paul[31] in chapter 2 gives a number of instructions related to appropriate behaviour. First, he instructs that prayer is made for everyone (2:1), and then he instructs both the men and the women as to what was fitting in prayer (2:8-10). We can assume that the instructions to the men and the women are in some way to counteract the false teachers as this is the purpose of the letter (1:3).[32] The word to the men ('to lift up holy hands in prayer without anger or disputing' - 1 Timothy 2:8) serves as a response to their controversies and strife, and it seems safe to assume that the word to the women ('to dress modestly... with good works....' - verses 9,10) likewise is to correct how this error had impacted them. His word to the women addresses appropriate dress

---

[31]For the sake of brevity I will refer to the author as Paul. If Paul did not write this pastoral then it is probable that one of his disciples wrote it. Either way the implied author is Paul and it is best to assume that the letter is at least Pauline. If it was proven that he was not the author then some of the arguments that follow might need to be modified, but the essential elements within them would remain the same.

[32]The letter is not a manual on church order, but a response to major problems of disorder caused by the spread of false doctrines.

and attitude. The verses that we will focus on, because of their controversial content, (verses 11-15) then follow.

2.2 Timothy 2:11-15: an absolute prohibition on women teaching?

Before turning directly to the text there are a number of aspects that I wish to explore, and if they are close to being accurate then a claim that these verses put forward a universal prohibition against women teaching would be most unlikely.

1. Timothy travelled with Paul and would have been well acquainted with Paul's teaching and practice. If Timothy was allowing women to teach at Ephesus this would be very surprising if he knew that Paul *never* allowed women to teach. If there was no possibility of women teaching at Ephesus then it seems unlikely that Paul would have made this statement here at all. It seems that either women were teaching and causing a problem or the threat of women teaching in this way was a very real one.[33]

2. If women were universally barred from teaching, it is rather surprising that Paul can acknowledge the important role that women had in teaching Timothy himself (2 Tim. 1:5; 3:15), or give encouragement to women to teach other women and children (2 Timothy 3:14; Titus 2:3-5). Although (rightly) it can be argued that these forms of teaching are different, if one of the reasons why women are forbidden to teach is that their gender is specially prone to deception, one would expect that this would affect women in *all* types of teaching.

3. Women were allowed to prophesy, which often includes inspired instruction, so why were they not allowed to instruct in other ways? Prophecy and teaching both need to be weighed against revealed

---

[33]And if the Pauline practice was to never allow women to teach it is surprising that this would be the only explicit Scriptural reference to it - unless it is argued that the combination of teaching and having authority over men is what Paul is prohibiting, rather than simply prohibiting teaching.

truth. We cannot argue that prophecy was to be weighed, but that the teacher was allowed to teach authoritatively without any checks and balances.[34]

4. There is no evidence that Paul ever sought to curtail Priscilla's involvement in teaching (and at certain stages of her life and ministry she was based in Ephesus).

So it is highly unlikely that Timothy has allowed (or is in danger of allowing) a situation to develop that Paul would have disapproved of, or that Paul himself is now taking an absolute stance against women teaching. It is unlikely, therefore, that these verses are pressing for a universal ban on all women teachers.

It is now to some comments on the text that we turn.

2.3 Comments on the text

In setting the scene we note that Paul instructs the whole church to pray (2:1) and then turns his attention toward the men in 2:8, encouraging them to direct their speech in prayer, rather than in anger or argument. So we have a mixture of universal command (prayer by all, for all in every place) and a specific local application to the Ephesian men. It is likely that the men were influenced by the false teaching (1:3) to express themselves in ways that lacked self-control, and it is easy to make a connection between the promotion of controversies / speculations mentioned in chapter 1 and the anger and disputing mentioned here.

He then comes to address the women in verse 9, opening with a word (*hosautos* — likewise, this being more specific than the English 'also') linking his instruction to them with his instruction to the men. The motivation behind these two comments are therefore similar and we

---

[34]Indeed one might wish to argue that far from Paul placing the (so-called) teaching office above that of the prophet comes unstuck on Paul's (hierarchical?) listing of apostle, prophet and teacher (1 Cor. 12:29). To argue as some have that prophecy is a non-authoritative proclamation is not at all convincing.

could almost translate the opening phrase of this verse as 'for the same reason'. It is then something of a surprise (to us) that he proceeds to address issues of dress. (This again indicates that although there is a universal command to pray, he is now giving localised instructions.) We can therefore conclude that, in some way, the modest dress of the women will be as appropriate as the peaceful prayer of the men, both being linked to counteracting the effect of the false teaching that Paul warns against in chapter 1.

Thus far we realise that both contentiousness (by the men) and extravagant dressing (by the women) will disturb the harmonious relationships to which the church is called. This raises the question as to how the dress code of these women could cause a problem. Fee notes that, 'There is a large body of evidence, both Hellenistic and Jewish, which equated dressing up on the part of women with both sexual wantonness and wifely insubordination. Indeed, for a married woman so to dress in public was tantamount to marital unfaithfulness.'[35]

It seems that the false teaching is expressing itself among the people with arguments and anger being displayed by the men and in some measure of insubordination, and perhaps even by a sexually inappropriate dress code, among the women. Paul then continues to address the women in verse 11 instructing that they learn quietly and in full submission, which stands in contrast to the lack of submission exhibited by the false teachers (1:9).

This then brings us to the verse which reads 'I permit no woman to teach or to have authority over a man, she is to keep silent'. A number of key points need to be noted here regarding translation.

Firstly, the translation of the word *hesuchia*, which appears in verse 11 and in verse 12. It is too strong to translate this word as

---

[35] *1 and 2 Timothy, Titus*, New International Biblical Commentary (Peabody: Hendrickson, 1988; Carlisle: Paternoster, 1995), p. 71.

absolute silence.[36] Translating it as 'quietness' seems most appropriate for that is in keeping with the thrust of Paul's words thus far. The women are to avoid behaviour that would cause a disturbance to harmonious relationships. Fee states that 'some kind of disruptive behaviour, which perhaps included boisterous affirmation of the heresies seem to lie behind these instructions'.[37]

Then, secondly, the translation of the word *authentein*. This word is used only this once in the New Testament (here) and is not the normal word for 'have authority' (*exousiazein*). In the light of the fact it is only rarely used outside the New Testament during this period, it is not easy to ascribe an exact meaning to the word. However, the parameters lie between the usage in the classical period (around 200BC) when it had associations with murder to the usage in the patristic period (around 200AD) when it simply meant to 'exercise authority'. Leland Wilshire has addressed this passage, and this word in particular, in a number of articles. In one such article, having laid out the historical occurrences of the word and its cognates over the four hundred years in question,[38] he concludes that, 'An analysis of this list shows that one can find very few citations during this four century period surrounding the New Testament that have the meaning of 'to hold sway or use power, to be dominant'... the preponderant number of citations

---

[36] 1 Tim. 2:2 translated as 'quiet' lives; 2 Thess. 3:12 'settle down'. Even if the word were to be translated as 'silence' I suggest that the same word, when it appears in the same context, should at least be translated the same way each time (the quietness of verse 11 and the silence of verse 12 (NIV) are the same word, *hesuchia*). There is a very big difference between absolute silence and an appropriate quietness in order to learn.

[37] Fee, p. 73.

[38] This was done using the computerised word-search facility of the 'Thesaurus Liguae Graeca' project (normally abbreviated to 'TLG'), based at the University of California. This project entered virtually the entire corpus of ancient Greek literature spanning some 63 million words, 3,000 authors and a 1,200 year period onto a computer database. Wilshire was then able to survey a total of 329 occurrences of *authentein* and its cognates.

from this compilation have to do with self willed violence, criminal action, or murder or with the person who does these actions.'[39] He then goes on to suggest that the word must carry the sense of 'instigating violence' in 1 Timothy 2:12. This meaning could either be literary hyperbole or, if intended literally, would indicate the gravity of the situation thus giving cause for his appeal for quietness.

My preference would be to understand the word as literary hyperbole as there seems to be no evidence of literal violence taking place in Ephesus (although this conceivably could be a parallel to the anger and arguments that the men are told to avoid). However we understand the word, Wilshire's point remains that the word carries considerably stronger connotations than simply that of 'authority'. I suggest therefore we are looking for a meaning that would communicate something along the line of 'self-willed behaviour' or 'domineer'.[40]

Another issue to settle is whether the prohibition against teaching is linked to the prohibition not to domineer over a man (or husband, the Greek word being the same for both). If this is so then it would not simply be a prohibition against all forms of teaching and in all contexts by women, but teaching that specifically fell into the category of teaching that domineered over men. It is not possible to be dogmatic but the use of the two infinitive verbs (and the parallels I will refer to below) suggest that they are linked together, with the second one qualifying the first one, thus we could read it as, 'I do not permit a woman to teach, that is in a way that domineers over a man'. Reading it this way also allows for the implicit, but very obvious, parallels between verses 11 and 12. The

---

[39] '1 Timothy 2:12 Revisited: A Reply to Paul W. Barnett and Timothy J. Harris', *Evangelical Quarterly*, Vol. LXV No. 1 (January 1993), p. 47.

[40] Keener, *Paul*, p. 109, notes that the word 'could well mean "domineer," since it is different from and probably stronger than the term he normally uses.' He also points out that in the context Paul will go on to invoke the Genesis language of Eve 'probably indicating that these women are not submitting to their husbands but rather are seeking to lord it over them.'

teaching aspect of verse 12 parallels the learning aspect of verse 11, while the domineering parallels that of *full* submission. She is to learn with certain attitudes and not to teach with certain attitudes. So the problem at Ephesus is not that women are teaching, but that they are teaching in a self-appointed fashion with little or no respect to conventions nor authority.[41] I would concur with Anderson's comments on this passage: 'It is not the question of instructing or teaching but the manner of doing it' which is in question in these verses.[42]

If the above is correct then we have a situation where the heretical teaching has impacted the women in such a way that they are domineering over men, and so Paul makes the forceful statement that he does not allow them to teach in that way (although even this statement needs to be balanced against his equally strong[43] statement that the women are to learn). He completes this section through a repetition of the noun 'quietness' thus making sure that his concern for the peaceful life in all godliness and dignity (2:2) is emphasised, and that his prohibitions are in order to counteract the disturbance of the harmony that has taken place through the heretical teachers in Ephesus.

We can outline the chiasmic shape[44] of these verses as follows:

---

[41]It is possible that the domineering was specifically aimed at their own husbands. The words *gune* and *aner* used here for woman / man respectively can also mean wife / husband. If there was a specific problem within marriage it would have been reflective of a more general problem within the church. I will seek to address it at this wider level.

[42]J. A. Anderson, 'Woman's warfare and ministry', *Christian Herald* (London, 1935), p. 30.

[43]Paul uses a verb in the imperative (command) mood in verse 11, 'let the women learn', thus placing great focus on this. In verse 12, he says 'I do not allow a woman to teach'. The strength of this verb is less than first verb, this one taking the indicative mood. Thus the focus seems to be on the former and not the latter verb.

[44]A chiasm is where a section of text is perceived to be in two halves, in which the second half mirrors the first one.

A Appropriate behaviour fitting godliness
    B To be in quietness
    C To learn in all submission

        C` Not to teach and domineer
    B` To be in quietness
A` Reasons for appropriate behaviour

Before turning to Paul's own justification for his words (verses 13-15, beginning with the word 'for') I would like now to present a possible scenario that has arisen.

2.4 The situation that Paul is addressing

If there is a situation in Ephesus where Paul is encouraging the women to be educated but restricting them from a teaching role, what would that situation be? I will outline below three suggested solutions with the final one being the one that seems to me to best fit the situation.

2.4.1 Uneducated women are teaching heresy

This solution is very attractive and, in summary, suggests that 1) the women were generally uneducated in society; 2) they have been liberated by the gospel to a place of equality alongside the men; 3) they then are using their equality to function alongside the men; but 4) their lack of knowledge meant that they were not equipped to teach. So 5) Paul forbids them to teach at this stage until, 6) they have been sufficiently educated when they themselves will be able to teach accurately. The three reasons that Paul then gives in verses 13-15 are understood as three reasons for his insistence on their education (Eve is part of creation, so don't exclude her from being taught; she was deceived in the fall, so we need to ensure that women are educated; and the promise of salvation came to her and was brought through the child promised as Eve's offspring — the Redeemer promised in Gen. 3:15 — so as fully part of the redeemed community women must not be excluded from the learning process).

Attractive as this solution is, it is highly unlikely that women who were uneducated and downtrodden as second-class, were transformed to such an extent that they broke out of their social and cultural background and came into the assembled body exerting themselves over men (or their husbands?). Also the revolutionary nature of the women being taught has been somewhat overstated. 'It is simply going to far to argue from this that he is herewith commanding that they be taught, thus inaugurating a new era for women. The rest of the data in the New Testament makes it clear that that had already happened among most Christians.'[45]

2.4.2 A Gnostic-type heresy

Richard Clark Kroeger and Catherine Clark Kroeger have built their case on the culture of first-century Ephesus suggesting that there is a Gnostic-type error that has taken root among women.[46] They argue, convincingly, that the Pastorals were written to oppose heresy, not to establish church behavioural norms with 1 Timothy directed against a Gnostic-type situation where women were being given an inordinate place. Written to Timothy in Ephesus which was 'a bastion of feminine supremacy in religion',[47] they note that Ephesus was the centre for the worship of Artemis (the Greek name for the same goddess that was known as Diana in Latin). Artemis was seen to be the mother of all gods and humanity, and this influence led to distortions of biblical teachings. One significant example of this being the exaltation of the serpent as the embodiment of a deity that was superior to Yahweh and the belief that Eve was superior to Adam

Verses 13-15 are then understood as giving a rationale to the prohibition of verse 12. The Gnostic-type heresy having exalted Eve,

---

[45]Fee, *1 Timothy*, p. 72.
[46]*I Suffer Not a Woman, Rethinking 1 Timothy 2:11-15 in Light of Ancient Evidence* (Grand Rapids: Baker, 1992).
[47]Ibid., p. 54.

and thereby women, as the originators[48] which Paul refutes from the Jewish tradition as represented in Genesis. Paul's prohibition is suggested as follows: 'I do not permit a woman to teach nor to represent herself as originator of man but she is to be in conformity [with the Scriptures]... For Adam was created first, then Eve.'[49] Thus Paul refutes any teaching that Eve was the source for Adam, or that it was Adam that was deceived.[50] And finally he gives value to childbearing which, along with marriage, the Gnostics had denigrated.

For those who wish to follow the argument through further, the book itself is commended and it has much to offer. In its defence, the Pastorals do contain many references which can easily be understood as directed to Gnostic-type practices and beliefs.[51] The weakness of this solution *might* lie in the reconstruction of the heresy as an exalted Gnostic or proto-Gnostic view of Eve, for we don't know how developed it would have been by this stage, and I do not consider that the analysis of *authentein* is as convincing as Wilshire's (referred to earlier in this chapter) who suggests it refer to violent action.[52] I wish to recommend their research, and will below present a slightly alternative reconstruction, which might be seen by others as less convincing!

---

[48]They understand the word *authentein* to convey the concept of origination, authorship or source of something.

[49]Ibid., p. 103.

[50]Paul states emphatically that Adam was *not* deceived, but that Eve was deceived. In Eve's case he even strengthens the verb 'deceive' with a prefix *ex*, thus removing any scope of pleading Eve's innocence. See, ibid., p. 123.

[51]So, for example, we have references to 'myths' (Tit. 1:14), 'old wives tales' (1 Tim. 4:7), 'meaningless talk' (1 Tim. 1:6) and false knowledge (*gnosis*) (1 Tim. 6:20).

[52]An omission of the Kroegers' work is that they do not interact with Wilshire's analysis. Their analysis would be more plausible if 1 Timothy was dated in the second century, a view held by some scholars, but not by the Kroegers.

2.4.3 Women of high social background have been deceived and are teaching

If the verses that immediately precede give us an indication of the women that are causing problems we would understand them to be from a well-to-do background.[53] The fact that they could be wearing gold or expensive clothes suggests this (2:9f.). This would indicate that they either belonged to the class that ran the city or were pretending to belong to that social class. These would not be the downtrodden slave-mentality women that were common in the wider culture, but would have been well equipped emotionally and socially to take on positions of authority. Such women, although having responded to the gospel, could well have continued with attitudes that were less than regenerate. Their previous life had not been one where they had learned 'quietly and in full submission', and in their over-confidence they were guilty of seizing authority. Paul therefore will not allow these women to teach with those attitudes, but insist that they learn with a corresponding godly attitude that would be 'appropriate for women who profess to worship God'.

I also suggest that the Artemis-background is a major factor. This female deity was worshipped as the virgin-huntress and venerated as the mother of all gods and humans. Her shrine dominated the Ephesian city with her Temple being one of the seven wonders of the ancient world and her cult wielded 'significant influence over the social, religious, economic and political lives of people throughout Asia Minor.'[54] Given that the rituals in these cults normally culminated in symbolic union with the deity, the dominance of the feminine in Ephesus is easy to understand. This dominance is further indicated in the priesthood that presided over the Temple activities, for this consisted of

---

[53]See the references in Acts which mention women of high standing either explicitly or implicitly: 13:50; 16:14 (Lydia); 17:4, 12, 34 (Damaris); 18:2-3, 18-26 (Priscilla).

[54]Clinton E. Arnold, *Powers of Darkness* (Downers Grove: IVP; Leicester: IVP, 1992), p. 207.

male eunuch-priests and three grades of priestesses.[55] This ancient cult then exalted the feminine and tended to emasculate the male.

Perhaps some of the women converts of high standing came directly from this background, but even if this was not the case, it is highly likely that they had been influenced. It is possible to read verse 12 as suggesting activity and attitudes that were parallel to that of the women involved in the Artemis cult. The converts, like the Artemis-women, were domineering and even emasculating men. It is to this situation that Paul speaks, stating in no uncertain terms that they are not to teach, domineering over men.

Now drawing from elements of the heretical teaching we can, from reading between the lines of the text, understand that their teaching had a strong ascetic thrust (1 Timothy 4:1-3) probably based on a claim that the resurrection had already taken place (2 Timothy 2:18). The ascetic element included a forbidding of marriage — perhaps because to marry was too acknowledge that one belonged to this age. (On these issues I am in strong agreement with the Kroegers that there clearly are Gnostic-type emphases involved.) These heretical teachers appear to have had particular success with certain women (2 Timothy 3:6).

Lloyd Pietersen, has (rightly) drawn attention to the material on widows in 1 Timothy 5:3-16 noting that the author devotes so much space to it.[56] He suggest that there were a number of younger widows who were now on the widow's list who were draining the material resources of the church (1 Timothy 5:16), but were also causing trouble within the church, for they were 'idle, gadding about from house to house; and... not merely idle, but also gossips and busybodies, saying what they should not say' (5:13).

---

[55]F. F. Bruce, *Acts*, New International Commentary of the New Testament (Grand Rapids: Eerdmans, 1954), pp. 397f.
[56]'Women and the Pastorals' *Anabaptism Today*, Issue 17 (Spring 1998), pp. 8-16, and Issue 18 (Summer 1998), pp. 15-19.

No longer being married (the meaning of having left their first pledge in 5:12 could be that they had left their husbands) they were now being encouraged by the false teachers to be released into 'ministry'. They were now free from the restraints that came through being part of the normal household structure. But from Paul's perspective this freedom had meant that some had already turned to follow Satan (5:15) and whatever ministry they were being encouraged to assert, Paul indicated that it was nothing more than gossip. In this context Paul insists that such widows be encouraged to 'marry, bear children and immerse themselves in their households'.[57]

Putting all the above together we now have a most plausible scenario: false teachers had infiltrated the community (indeed some of the teachers might have once been leaders within the community) and had great success among younger women, many of whom were from a wealthy background. The teaching was gnostic in part, with a strong emphasis on asceticism and specifically abstinence from marriage. Some of these widows had possibly even divorced their husbands in order to fully participate in the resurrection experience. They were now self appointed teachers of these truths. We do not know exactly what the teaching was but with the Artemis-type background (and looking at what Paul is about to say in 2:13-15) it was almost certainly to do with the over-exaltation of women and a corresponding emasculation of men. The church is facing a major crisis (one which Paul himself had prophesied would take place in Acts 20:29,30) and only drastic action will bring things back in line. Hence the solution offered by Paul in 2:13-15 (and for the younger widows in 5:14-16) is both extreme and *also local*. It is not one which we could insist is made into a universal law — if we were to do so, we should also be consistent and insist on no hair braiding, wearing of gold, or expensive clothes (2:9-10), or that all younger widows in our day and culture also remarry, for this is what the apostle wants (5:14 same word as in 2:8 *boulomai*, 'I want').

---

[57]Pietersen, 'Women', p. 11.

It is then to this specific and localised situation that Paul is saying that he does not allow a woman to teach and domineer over a man, although he does insist that she learn. He then draws on three aspects, mainly from Genesis, to validate his prohibition. His appeal is to three elements: the order of creation, the deception within the fall and a strange reference to 'salvation through childbirth'. If the appeal to the chronological priority of Adam over Eve in creation is the basis for a universal ban on women teaching (as some traditionalists claim) that would be most surprising, for to do so would be to deduce much more from those creation passages than they yield exegetically. Likewise, for Paul to claim that male superiority is to be advanced in the church because of the fall is again to miss the mark, for Paul's gospel declares that a connection with Adam has been broken through our union with Christ.

Here the suggestions by the Kroegers are at the very least plausible and worthy of our consideration. If the false teachers have been teaching 'myths and endless genealogies that promote speculations' (1:4) it is not unlikely that they had been promoting a new genealogy, one where Eve was formed first rather than Adam.[58] If this is so, then his appeal is not to a creation order to justify a ban on women teaching, his appeal is rather to the Hebrew Scriptures to establish truth and expose the error of what has been taught. Likewise, his appeal to the fall would not be to establish the proneness to deception by (all) women, but would in order to establish that the woman was not an innocent party — she fell into transgression having been deceived. (Perhaps these women were also making the claim that they were vehicles of special revelation — Paul then warns them that the first

---

[58]Timothy J, Harris, 'Why did Paul mention Eve's Deception: A Critique of P. W. Barnett's Interpretation of 1 Timothy 2' in *Evangelical Quarterly*, Vol. LXII / No. 4 (Oct., 1990), p. 345, says that there is 'ample evidence of Jewish and gnostic speculations about Eve, which included the notion that she took part in the creation of the world and pre-existed Adam.'

woman was totally deceived.) The tragedy in Ephesus was that this historic fact was being replayed again in their very midst with the women being deceived. The women were claiming special revelation but Paul says they were actually being deceived. The deception is not a minor one but total.

The third factor could be a promise of salvation through the birth of the Messiah (as noted above with an appeal to Genesis 3:15) but Pietersen notes the parallel to 1 Timothy 5:14 where Paul encourages widows to marry and bear children.[59] It seems most likely that we have a reference to bearing children rather than any subtle reference to the birth of Christ. This can be understood against the background of either the abandonment or the despising of marriage through the false teaching. Paul wants to reassure the women, that contrary to the false teaching, salvation does not require the abandonment of normal duties in order to know Christ, rather such duties are perfectly in line with salvation, indeed fulfilling such duties is fitting for women who profess godliness (2:10) and will give the adversary no means by which to oppose them (5:14). If Eve was 'cursed' through childbirth these women can find immense blessing in that context provided they continue in the appropriate heart responses of 'faith and love and holiness, with modesty'.[60]

Pietersen takes the suggestion one step further by saying that he considers in this context that salvation is a saving from error. By following these instructions they will not be vulnerable to deception. He appeals to 1 Timothy 4:16 as a parallel where we read that Paul

---

[59]Pietersen, 'Women', p. 9. He notes that in 5:14 we have *teknogonein*, a verb and in 2:15 we have *teknogonia*, a related noun. This is the only occurrences of these in the NT.

[60]If the false teachers were also using the Gen. 3:16 text to indicate that Eve was cursed in childbearing that would be further ammunition for them to suggest that the women should avoid marriage and any motherly function. Paul then would be directly counteracting that here.

instructs Timothy, 'Pay close attention to yourself and to your teaching; continue in these things, for in doing this you will save both yourself and your hearers.' There the salvation being referred to is a salvation from error.

Again in conclusion, even if the various reconstructions suggested above remain unconvincing, we are still left with Paul essentially addressing a specific situation at a specific time. 'This text illustrates that there are times when the pastoral problems faced by the church are of such magnitude that some clear principles (here, the egalitarian position of Gal. 3:28) have to be modified for a time in the light of other principles (here, safeguarding the church from error) in order to deal with the problems at hand.'[61] To make this text into a universal prohibition against women would be to build a large construction on a very small foundation.

3. Restrictive passages: how restrictive?

In this chapter I have sought to demonstrate that the passages used to restrict women can be read in a way that does not restrict women. I am sure, given the complex nature of all three passages, that my interpretation will not have convinced all. I do not believe that an interpretation that satisfies all is possible to discover, but again I want to underline that the nature of these texts mean that we are ultimately dealing with instructions to a specific place at a specific time to deal with a specific situation. The onus, therefore, is on those who wish to restrict women to show that these verses should be universally applied.

Before moving on to the next chapter there are two other factors, and one other passage I wish to comment on briefly.

3.1 Issues in translation

It is important that we are aware of a number of factors that affect translation and can give a more strongly masculine bias within our Bibles

---

[61]Pietersen, 'Women' (Part 2), p. 17f.

than should be present. The use of the word *adelphoi* (brothers) throughout Scripture was not used to indicate that only men were being addressed (hence many translations use the inclusive term 'brothers and sisters'). This is reflective of a broader principle in the Greek language: if feminine terms are used this indicates an exclusive reference to women, whereas if masculine terms are used this does not necessarily mean that only men are in view. A third aspect is the need to distinguish the two Greek words, *anthropos* and *aner*, when translating. The former word is the general word for 'humanity, humankind, person, mortal, etc.', although *at times* it can mean 'male', it is the latter word that is specifically male. In translation, therefore, it is unnecessary to translate 2 Timothy 2:2 as: 'And the things you have heard me say in the presence of many witnesses entrust to faithful men (*anthropos*) who will also be qualified to teach others.' To translate this as 'men' is misleading. Perhaps worse still is the NIV translation of Hebrews 13:17 as, 'Obey your leaders and submit to their authority. They keep watch over you as men who must give an account.' The Greek does not use the word *anthropos* nor the word *aner*, but simply a masculine plural participle which in fairness should be translated generically neutral '...people who must give an account'. (The only reason to translate it specifically as male would be to reflect a prior judgement that leaders were male.)

3.2 What about women elders?

Although there are no women specifically mentioned as elders in the New Testament, it also needs to be remembered that only Peter and John are specifically mentioned by name as elders. If there were women in eldership, the omission of specific names is therefore not too surprising. Again, given that the expectation within New Testament culture probably was that the elders were more likely to be men does not give any indication to us today as to our expectation. Unless women are specifically restricted we should look to include them.

The main Pauline text on the qualifications for elders is found in 1 Timothy 3:1-7.[62] As noted above there are some eleven occasions when the Greek text is translated by the NIV in masculine terms, although it is in fact ambiguous. The text begins with the general statement that 'if *anyone* desires...' Although it is true that, given the culture, most elders were male, the text itself does not rule out the possibility of women elders. Within the Pauline qualifications there is only one aspect that is specifically masculine: it is the requirement that an overseer was to be 'husband of but one wife'. Although this could be in order to specifically indicate that women cannot qualify, I suggest for a number of reasons this is unlikely. If Paul intended these requirements (in verses 2-7) to be fulfilled in a literal fashion then they would also indicate that no single male could be an overseer (thus excluding perhaps Paul, Timothy, and certainly Jesus from ever fulfilling such a role!). It might also exclude someone who has been widowed. Again, given the qualifications regarding the children of overseers, the husband in a childless partnership would also not qualify (3:4). It is more likely that Paul intends to indicate the standard expected which Timothy was then to apply in an appropriate way. It seems far better to take it in the sense of '*if* married then... and *if* they have children then...'[63] Later, we read that deacons too are to be 'the husband of but one wife' (3:12), yet the preceding verse is most likely a reference to qualifications that should be applied to female deacons.[64] This would indicate that Paul did not intend

---

[62]I take the terms 'overseer' and 'elder' to be synonymous. It is only in the post-NT era that they were separated out. For our purposes it is immaterial whether they are one or two offices. Even if they are separate both are key leadership positions within the church.

[63]The emphasis of the phrase 'husband of one wife' is of the need for marital fidelity. Paul is indicating the need for exemplary marriage.

[64]Although it could be a reference to the wives of deacons as in the NIV, it would also be possible to see it as a reference to female overseers or deacons. So Paul gives qualifications of overseers and of deacons, with a specific mention of the women who would qualify before completing his comments on deacons. The

us to understand his comments about the men being married to one wife as meaning that women were excluded. Even if the reference here is to the wives of deacons, we know from the situation with Phoebe that she served as a deacon within the church at Cenchrea. So the only specifically masculine qualification should not be used in a literalistic way that then excludes women.

There might be a number of possibilities why Paul uses this masculine qualification. The most likely scenario is that by giving the masculine example, the reader understood that the feminine equivalent could be substituted. Had Paul used the feminine example this would have *explicitly excluded* the masculine equivalent, but by using the masculine example this would have *implicitly included* the feminine equivalent. Paul could have gone on and given the feminine example but this would have been superfluous.[65]

3.3 Women should obey: 1 Peter 3:1-7

There are similarities between this text and the Pauline instructions relating to appearance in 1 Timothy 2:9,10. Peter, like Paul, appeals to the women to have an inner 'unfading beauty of a gentle and quiet spirit' (verse 4). He then goes on to illustrate this with a call for them to emulate the holy women of the past, and uses Sarah as a prime example who 'obeyed Abraham and called him her master' (verse 6). This Scripture has been used to defend the authority of husbands and the need for wives to submit, and has even been pushed further to indicate that wives are to *obey* their husbands, even if what they were being required to do was wrong. The argument goes that the wife answers to the husband and in obeying her husband is in fact obeying God; the husband in turn answers to God and if he abuses his position he will be

---

specific mention of the type of women would be most appropriate in the light of the earlier discussions on the women that were causing problems in Ephesus.
[65]The phraseology might be pressed to mean that he is safeguard against polygamy, but as this was so rare, this is unlikely.

judged. The wife therefore owes obedience to her husband irrespective of his requests.

If this were the case, the nature of authority (as discussed in chapter 1) would be called into question. There we saw that authority was delegated and that within the human spheres no-one could demand absolute obedience. At a point of moral conflict, one's obedience had to be to God and Scripture. Two factors within this Petrine text will show that he does not have an absolute obedience in mind. First, it has a missionary setting for the appeal to submissive behaviour is in order that 'if any of them do not believe the word, they may be won over without words' (verse 1). Secondly, the obedience is counterbalanced by the requirement that the wives 'do not give way to fear' (verse 6). Only then will they be truly daughters of Sarah. One example from the life of Sarah indicates that she did not allow her submission to her husband to become one of fear: she insisted on the sending of Ishmael away from their family unit (Genesis 21:8-13). She refused to yield when she knew that she was in the right, and in spite of the tension that ensued, she insisted on holding her ground. Her obedience was anything but absolute at this point! In fact if there was obedience involved it was Abraham's, who was told to, 'Listen to whatever Sarah tells you' (Genesis 21:12).

To take this verse as a proof text that wives owe unqualified obedience to their husbands is to remove it from the context of the rest of Scripture, and indeed from the historical allusions that Peter himself makes. Peter ends with a plea for husbands and wives to live together in harmony. He addresses the husbands in verse 7, instructing them to live with their wives in a considerate way. Although they might be the weaker partner (perhaps meaning that they are in the weaker position within their culture due to the inferior view of women), as far as the gospel is concerned they are equally heirs before God. If the husbands abuse their position, then they will find that their prayers are hindered.

For Such A Time As This

Having examined various texts that could be used to restrict women, I suggest that the onus is on those who wish to place boundaries around women, that are different to the boundaries around men, to prove their point. It seems to me that Scripture does not forbid an equal function for women, so who are we to place upon them such restrictions?

CHAPTER 7

JESUS: THE MALE REDEEMER

If we accept the equality of men and women, particularly when we take a Christological and eschatological viewpoint,[1] we have not fully removed every difficult concept from the Bible relating to women as equal partners. Perhaps the most difficult is the apparent dominance of male imagery in Scripture. This apparent male dominance is evident when male terminology for God is predominantly used in Scripture, and when the Messiah appears, not simply in human likeness, but in male flesh.[2] These two aspects will be considered for they have been taken to imply female subordination and inequality. I, however, suggest that it is important for these male images to be present in Scripture in order to reveal the redemptive nature of God for the human race, and will argue that they do not imply inequality for women. Therefore my suggestion is that the weighting of male imagery, far from undermining the equality of the genders, is in fact necessary when interpreted from a redemptive viewpoint.

1.   Modifying the imagery

The above imagery can be modified fairly easily. As is often pointed out, the male imagery of God is not something which is exclusive. Yahweh is

---

[1] A Christological viewpoint means that we consider the revelation of God in Christ and how that impacts our perspective on men and women, who are both in Christ; and by taking an eschatological viewpoint this implies that we do not simply consider the new humanity in Christ as belonging to this creation but to the new creation. In Christ men and women are already experiencing the realities of the coming age in part, and their status and relationships must reflect that.

[2] If we had not already covered the issue of the twelve male apostles and the 'headship' of men within the marriage relationship, we would have added those issues here.

portrayed in female roles within the Old Testament. He[3] is someone who supplies water for Israel, feeds the people with manna, and clothes the human family. Other maternal imagery includes the carrying and care for the sucking child, or, even more poignantly, Yahweh is like a woman in travail who brings Israel to birth.[4] Jesus also, by implication, likened God to a woman sweeping her house clean until she found the lost coin. Although other similar imagery could be added, we are still left with an overwhelming tendency of the Bible to use male imagery to describe God.

Noting that there is female imagery used to describe God within Scripture should at least restrain us from holding solely to a male concept of God. God is surely neither male nor female (but arguably both masculine and feminine) and therefore any reaction to describing God as 'she' needs to be weighed very carefully. If, however, we accept that there is considerably more male imagery and language[5] than there is female in the Bible, is there a way that the material can be approached which does not point toward male supremacy?

When the time comes for Messiah to be revealed, the birth is through a woman but the child born is male. Jesus was clearly revolutionary in the way that he treated women within his culture. As seen in chapter 3, Jesus had women followers at one level or another; he

---

[3]Tempted as I might be to use the pronoun 'she' or to write 's/he' I am aware that would be misleading. The feminine pronouns indicate a femaleness that would be inaccurate. We cannot bring correction by changing our concepts of God to a goddess. Although the masculine pronouns do not indicate that God is male, I will continue to use them. Such is the limitation of language.

[4]See for instance the citations of feminine imagery for God in Leonard Swidler, *Biblical Affirmations of Women* (Philadelphia: Westminster Press, 1979), pp. 21-36; and in Mary Evans, *Woman*, pp. 21f.

[5]We need to point out that a word's grammatical gender does not necessarily denote the gender of the being it refers to. God and humankind are both masculine in the Greek and Hebrew languages and therefore any pronouns related to those words will be masculine. Nothing can be inferred regarding God's actual gender simply because the pronouns used are in the masculine gender.

performed women's tasks and he gladly gave women time and counted them worthy of discipleship. However, we are still left with a male Messiah.

2. Proposed approach

I suggest that we cannot simply sweep aside the apparent dominance of the male imagery within Scripture, but that, perhaps, we can look for an explanation for this bias other than the concept of male superiority. The basic proposal will be that there is a redemptive principle at work which is underlined by the male imagery. We will look at applying this proposal to both areas beginning with the maleness of Jesus. We begin with Christ for he is the model for true humanity and the true revelation of God (to which Scripture bears witness). We can only understand God and humanity in the light of God's self-disclosure in Jesus.[6]

2.1 Jesus — the Male Redeemer

Jesus was not one who endorsed ongoing patriarchal dominance, yet a crucial question remains which we can summarise as, 'could the Messiah have taken on female flesh?'. Is it as simple as the issue that: for Jesus to appear in first-century Jewish culture and live as a female Messiah (the Daughter of God) calling Yahweh her Mother would have been unthinkable?[7] Or is it that there is more to it than this simple perspective?

If the witness of Scripture primarily reflects the story of God's redemptive work within history, then we note that male dominance is part of the history of the fallen human race. Genesis 3:16 ('but your husband will rule over you') can be taken to speak of the sad state of affairs resulting from the Fall and to be an accurate record of male dominance throughout human history. To borrow phraseology and concepts from the Theology of Liberation: men have been the

---

[6]By so doing I am proposing a Christo-centric hermeneutic. In this particular sphere of discussion (male superiority) I suggest that this must be the best hermeneutic.

[7]See C. Norman Krauss, *Savior*, pp. 95-96 for this suggestion.

oppressors and women the oppressed throughout history. If this assessment is correct (both historically and theologically) we need to apply the theological principle of God's bias toward the oppressed to the male/female relationship.[8] Boldly, therefore, we can state that God has been on the side of women. This then I believe is the key to unlock the reason for God revealing Messiah in male flesh.

My own thinking on this issue began when I was gently challenged by a man in an audience I had been addressing on the subject of women in the Bible. He suggested that I was verging on hypocrisy by addressing the subject, and if I really believed what I was teaching I would be giving that particular session to a woman to address. The provocation coincided with some research into Liberation Theology which I realised was addressing this very situation. I perceived that they had rightly understood that God was on the side of the oppressed (the poor), but was not convinced that God addressed his word to them in order that they might rebel. The word of the Lord seemed to come to the oppressors (the rich) and demand that they deal justly. His word came to those with the power and that had the voice so as they could repent, lifting up the broken and oppressed through servanthood, humility and the sharing of resources. This gave me a conviction that I needed to continue to speak out for those who were oppressed: to model a release of the powerless. It was this challenge that caused me to view Jesus in a new light and to gain fresh insight into his maleness.

For the powerless (in our study, women) to speak out for equality can soon be dismissed as coming from vested interest, or worse still as 'rebellious'. It rather requires the one with the voice to speak up and make a call for the release of those that have been marginalised. It was this model that I then applied to Jesus and his maleness.

---

[8]The announcement of liberation to the oppressed comes to a climax in the ministry and work of Jesus (Luke 4:17-20), but is clearly traced throughout the Old Testament, and in particular with the denouncement of injustice in the prophetic writings.

Jesus comes in the form of the oppressor but identifies with the oppressed. He comes in the form of the gender who has power, but uses the position of privilege to elevate and liberate those without power and privilege.[9] He models true redemption, for redemption does not begin with the oppressed throwing off the shackles of the oppressor, but with full and complete repentance being undertaken by the oppressor. When this repentance principle is absent, history records that the oppressed in a given situation tend to seek their own liberation — often through violent means. Although this cannot be justified, neither can the continuation of oppression. Some might argue that revolution is better than oppression, but true redemption surpasses any form of revolution, and it is true and full redemption that Christ came to bring.

So the only way to bring about change for a female Messiah would be to respond in rebellion. If, however, the female Messiah did not respond in rebellion but lived a self-sacrificing life, such as we see in Jesus, Stanley Grenz suggests that her life and ministry would merely have been interpreted as the ideal role for all women within society. There would have been nothing counter-cultural about such activity, and the status quo would have remained. But Jesus, as male, was counterculture and his maleness 'was an indispensable dimension of his vocation'.[10]

---

[9]This same principle is seen in other aspects of the life of Jesus. He was a Jew but did not exclude others. Rather he used his status in a redemptive way so as there might no longer be Jew nor Greek in the new humanity. He was the Lord of all but used his lordship to become the servant of all so as there might be the end of the class barrier of slave and free. He laid aside wealth for our sake and did not avail himself of political power for his own ends. In short he never used his privileges to endorse any form of hierarchy. In different ways he had the opportunity to do so but at every turn refused to follow the cultural norms of his day. In this way he refused to submit to the sin of oppression but became the liberator of those who were oppressed.

[10]Grenz, *Theology for the Community of God* (Carlisle: Paternoster Press, 1994), p. 378.

Jesus identifies with the human race in its sinfulness,[11] and specifically with males in their sin of oppression and exploitation, through taking on male flesh. He refuses to insist on his male prerogatives, but lays them down as the Servant-redeemer. In so doing he is not only redeeming humanity in general but is also redeeming maleness, for he demonstrates not simply the image for true humanity, but the image for true maleness. Gone is the image of one who dominates; centre-stage appears the image of a man who sides with the oppressed and becomes a voice for them. Gone is the image of the male who lives to exert his will; centre-stage is the true male who reveals that true identity is found in doing the will of God.[12] Only in Jesus is true maleness revealed — he is the redeeming image for men.

Yet there is more to the redemptive imagery of the male redeemer, for Jesus is also the redemptive image for women. If men and women together are to fulfil the purposes of God,[13] it is necessary for women to see in the new humanity a new model of maleness. In Jesus, who is the head of this new race, that model is clear. Those who have been oppressed (females) can now trust the oppressor (males) as they are conformed to his image. Only through repentance by the oppressor can trust be restored and the partnership of equals be truly initiated. Had Messiah come in the form of female flesh, vicarious 'repentance' by the oppressor would not have been possible. The giving away of privilege and power would not have been possible and equality could only have

---

[11]Jesus was in 'the form of sinful flesh' (Rom. 8:3) and underwent the baptism of John to indicate that he was identifying with the human race rather than standing apart from it (Matt. 3:15).

[12]Jesus clearly underlined that woman's call was not in the bearing of children but in following God as a disciple (Luke 11:27,28). He stood apart from the rabbis of his day through the elevation of women alongside men.

[13]The cultural mandate of Gen. 1:26-28 was given to humankind equally as male and female. This commission to rule was tied up with being created in the image of God. In the new humanity again both males and females are being conformed to the image of the Son, thus qualifying them together to fulfil the cultural mandate through the Gospel.

been restored through rebellion, which is not the way of our redeemer God. Jesus is (and indeed must be) male in order to redeem both males and females through his life as well as his death.

The quote from Grenz below is a helpful summary of the liberating impact of the maleness of Christ on both males and females.

> Jesus liberated males from the role of domination that belongs to a fallen world, in order that they can be truly male... As a male, Jesus revealed that the way to life does not lie in acting the part of the strong, dominating and self-sufficient male.

> The male Jesus liberated women as well, however. On their behalf he acted as the paradigm human standing against the male system. He brought them to participate in the new order where sex distinctions no longer determine rank and worth. As the author of their faith, the New Human, he provided resources to leave the past behind — to forgive and to be forgiven — and to seek the new order in which supplementarity is the rule.[14]

2.2 God as Male

Having begun with Jesus, let us now apply this redemptive principle to the male imagery of God. The male imagery of God, although not exclusive, is predominant in Scripture and therefore needs to be taken seriously.[15] Before we look at the possibility of there being a redemptive principle involved in such language we can take an intermediate step of seeking to determine what such male imagery would have communicated within the early biblical (and patriarchal) culture.

---

[14]*Theology*, p. 379.

[15]A point that should not be overlooked is the revelation of God's essential being and character to Moses (Exod. 3:14) employs no noun, proper or common, but simply the first person (genderless) singular verb.

It can be argued that male terminology would not have communicated maleness but transcendence.[16] In the ancient Near Eastern culture the gods and goddesses promoted the fertility of all life — the crops, flocks and families. They were intimately tied in with nature and the seasons, but Israel's God stood above nature. Goddess imagery would have communicated this intimate involvement with and even dependence on nature (mother nature?).[17] Even a male god with a female consort would have tied deity to the cycles of nature. However a male God who stood alone communicated total transcendence and Yahweh as the 'wholly other'. As Finger says:

> But what about a "masculine" God without a consort, who created and changed things simply by his "word" and acts? Such imagery was almost unique, and well suited to the God who had begun transforming nature and society — including its patriarchal structures.[18]

Likewise Dale Youngs says,

> The biblical message is clear: there is no multiplicity of divinities; God needs no female partner to perform the sex act with him, thereby giving birth to the earth and its creatures; God is above the condition of sexuality. When it comes to goddess worship, the whole tenor of the Hebrew Scriptures is open hostility.[19]

Once the transcendence of God is established in the history of Israel, we find an increasing number of female imageries which come through in the

---

[16]See Thomas N. Finger, *Christian Theology*, Vol. 2 (Scottdale: Herald, 1989), p. 485-490.

[17]A female goddess giving birth to creation might lead to creation and the goddess being of the same substance. Creation would be deified (and therefore worshipped) by such imagery. The God of the Bible appears as committed to creation, but distinct from it.

[18]*Theology*, Vol. 2, p. 486.

[19]'What's So Good About the Goddess?', *Christianity Today* (August 16, 1993), p. 21.

later writings. This transcendent God is the One who has chosen to be involved in an intimate way with her people. Certainly the imagery related to the Holy Spirit might indeed prompt us to refer to God as 'she' whenever we speak of that aspect of the work of the Trinity.[20]

This leaves us with the one important image of God as 'father'. Jesus' did not relate to God as an overpowering deity who needed to be appeased, and the deity with whom he had such an intimate relationship he revealed as 'father'. Indeed the intimacy of the relationship was such that we can see that there are as many motherly aspects in the heart of God as fatherly.[21] Jesus' use of the term 'father' communicated the sovereign, liberating, compassionate dimensions of God, but in a way which was far from endorsing stereotyped male models of fatherhood. We could argue that indeed the term 'father' could well have been deliberately chosen by Jesus to combat sexism. He injected the term 'father' with new meaning and so revealed a picture of fatherhood that does not endorse male dominance and patriarchal hierarchy. True fatherhood contains as many feminine attributes as it does masculine ones.[22]

Theologically God is portrayed in male terms to communicate his transcendence. And from a redemptive perspective, God is

---

[20]It has been argued that the work of the Spirit is one of bringing to birth and of nurturing and therefore feminine terms are more appropriate. The criticism from the feminist theologians that using exclusively male language for God conveys the impression that the human male is more God-like, than the female, needs to be taken seriously.

[21]Kenneth Leech has suggested that once the motherly aspects of God are lost that it can give rise to the Mother of God (mariolatry). See R. P. Stevens, 'The mystery of male and female: biblical and trinitarian models', *Themelios,* Vol. 17.3 (April/May 1992), p.21.

[22]See Robert Hamerton-Kelly, *God the Father: Theology and Patriarchy in the Teaching of Jesus* (Philadelphia: Fortress Press, 1979), pp. 21-36 and 357-359. Bearing in mind that Jewish culture was patriarchal, it is natural for Jesus to present God in a culturally relevant way; however he also greatly modifies the common Jewish concept.

portrayed as male, not to endorse continued male dominance, but to bring males in line with true maleness. Perhaps for males the Scripture, 'Be perfect as your Father in heaven is perfect', carries the added dimension of acting responsibly and redemptively in the area of male/female relationships.

Excursus: God, feminine imagery and male language

Alongside the male language we also have a considerable amount of feminine imagery applied to God that firmly prevents us from understanding God as male.

1. Yahweh is described as fulfilling roles that women had in ancient society: he provides food, water and clothing.[23]

2. Feminine images are used to provide comparisons to God: a mother bird and a mistress (in the sense of a woman in charge of servants).[24]

3. He is described in motherly terms: as a woman in labour; as a mother who will not forget her child; as the mother of Israel; and as a midwife.[25]

4. The compassion of God (Hebrew *rachim*) is essentially a feminine term from the Hebrew word for 'womb' (*rechem*). Likewise the Hebrew word *ruach* (Spirit) is feminine.

The feminine imagery means we cannot think of God in male terms; however the Bible avoids using female language as the God of Scripture is not female. If God had been known as 'mother' we would not only have goddess theology, but creation itself would be divine,

---

[23]Food — Exod. 16:4-36; Ps. 36:8; Hos. 11:4; water — Neh. 9:15; Exod. 17:1-17; clothing — Neh. 9:21.

[24]Bird — Ps. 17:8; 36:8; mistress in Ps. 123:2 (and also as a master in this verse).

[25]Labour — Is. 42:14; mother and child — Is. 49:15; 66:13; Yahweh as Israel's mother — Num. 11:2; Deut. 32:18 (also described as Israel's father in this verse); midwife — Ps. 22:9; 71:6; Is. 66:9.

having been given birth to by this deity. If God is identified with creation in such a way, we finally make ourselves into gods and goddesses. The Scripture avoids the possibility of this error and the rejection of goddess worship ultimately comes form understanding that Creator and created are separate.

Hence Scripture gives us the sensitive balance. It uses male language to communicate God's 'wholly otherness', his transcendence and distinction from creation — the God of the Bible is not dependent on creation. Yet this language is beautifully balanced by the feminine imagery which enables us not to fall into the trap of seeing God as male. This imagery however does not slip over into making God female, as the 'rejection of goddess worship ultimately comes from understanding that Creator and created are separate.'[26] Thus we have a God that is beyond male and female, yet embraces the masculine and feminine in each of us.

End of Excursus

Excursus: Trinitarian theology

The doctrine of the Trinity has been advanced in a hierarchical way (God the Father as the initiator / source / head of Christ) and has been used in a way to underline the rightness of a hierarchical relationship between men and women. Understanding the inter-relationships of the persons within the Trinity is a major task which theologians constantly seek to find fresh language to express, and I do not intend to suggest that I have any new understanding to bring. However, I do want to indicate that there are other ways of expressing those inter-relationships. I recently came across, in Miroslav Volf's outstanding book on the church, the following discussion.[27] (The passage quoted is part of a

---

[26]Youngs, 'Goddess?', p. 21.
[27]*After Our Likeness: The Church as the Image of the Trinity* (Grand Rapids: Eerdmans, 1998). Another example of a considerably less hierarchical model is found in Thomas Finger's *Christian Theology*, Vol. 2, pp. 379-406, 433-456. Two

larger discussion, and given the nature of the book, contains considerable technical language. However, the important point to grasp is his suggestion that the traditional discussions on 'being' and 'substance' do not necessarily make any statement on the relational level of the Trinity.)

> The constitution of persons through generation and procession grounds the distinctions among the persons, who are simultaneously constituted as standing in relations; these distinctions then manifest themselves in the salvation-historical differentiation of the persons.

> If this distinction between the "hypostatic divinity" (constitutional level) of the trinitarian persons and their "intertrinitarian form" (relational level) is persausive, then the unilinear hierarchical relations can disappear from the trinitarian communion, since maintaining that the Father constitutes the Son and Spirit says nothing as yet about *how* the relations between them are structured. In any case, within salvation history they do appear as persons standing in reciprocal relationships to one another... Moreover, within a community of perfect love between persons who share all the divine attributes, a notion of hierarchy and subordination is inconceivable.[28]

Thus using theological language and models, Volf makes the appeal that we must not confuse the means of being (even here language presents us

---

quotes will not do justice to these chapters, but will have to suffice: 'The divine "substance" is not a quantity handed down form one level to another. It is an energy ceaselessly flowing among, and continually revitalized by, different sources.' (p. 448). 'In itself, then the Trinity is not structured hierarchically. Thus this doctrine hardly implies that the church or society ought to be. On the contrary, it implies that the church and society should be structured as mutually as possible, with authority flowing back and forth among different but equally valuable persons and groups.' (p. 450).

[28] *After Our Likeness*, p. 217.

with difficulty, for such language can seem to imply that Son and Spirit become something they were not, which would be an enormous error) with modes of relating. The Son and the Spirit are constituted by the Father, who is the source of their divinity, but the Trinitarian form of God is determined by the mutuality of relationships.[29]

Thus using such a model of the Trinity and making an application to humanity would be to emphasise the interdependence of the genders, and the need for mutuality to be expressed. Something less than this would be to deny humanity the possibility of imaging the eternal God.

End of Excursus

2.3 Conclusions and summary

Redemption takes place within history and includes the redemption of relationships. Jesus is a male redeemer because of the history of male oppression. God is a father because patriarchal society and male leadership needs to be redeemed. A new model of leadership, which is neither male nor female, but both masculine and feminine (both fatherly and motherly) is necessary. The revelation of God as father redeems true leadership which is neither male nor female but partnership. If the husband as head means that he has a primary role of leadership within the family, then it would follow that he is the one who, in the area of his family, also has the primary responsibility to enact redemption. Because of male language within Scripture and Jesus the male redeemer, men and husbands can uniquely begin to reverse the tide of history. This is true redemption.

---

[29]This mutuality is well summed up in the Greek concept of the *perichoresis* of the Trinity — the concept that the mutuality and interpenetration within the Trinity being likened to the Godhead being involved in an eternal 'dance', one which humanity and all creation are being asked to join in. (This theme is developed well by Clark Pinnock and undergirds his social Trinitarian view, giving his Spirit in Creation material a very creative (no pun intended) feel — see *Flame of Love*.)

God is a redeemer. Yahweh frees the oppressed but calls for the oppressor (males) to repent. Through describing the self-revelation of the God, who is beyond gender, in male terms (though not exclusively) Yahweh has led the way for liberation. Male terminology might be open to abuse and misunderstanding, but it is also part of the process of redemption. Yahweh and Jesus often appear in the outward 'form' of the oppressor (the male) but identify with the oppressed. Surely as male followers of Jesus, men and husbands need to do likewise.

Terminology can at times be unhelpful and perhaps it is time to seek for new language which will help communicate the truths of Scripture within our culture. Perhaps we need to be more open to using 'she', when appropriate, as the masculine pronoun often now carries exclusive connotations.[30] Perhaps even new pronouns need to be coined which will help us communicate the transcendent God's journey with us through life.[31] Whatever our approach to the issue of terminology, we must be committed to going beyond terminology to discover and then apply the redemptive nature of God's revelation in all of our relationships.

---

[30]Historically the masculine pronouns have had an inclusive use, unlike the feminine pronouns. However this is increasingly becoming less true and if we insist on continuing to use exclusively masculine pronouns we might simply be adding to the confusion. Unfortunately, simply changing from masculine pronouns to corresponding feminine ones does not bring a solution, for those feminine pronouns have been historically even more exclusive than the masculine ones.

[31]Thomas N. Finger, *Theology*, Vol. 2, pp. 488-450, suggests the use of 'Godself' to avoid saying 'himself' or 'herself' when referring to God.

CHAPTER 8

FOR SUCH A TIME AS THIS

In this final chapter I simply want to summarise our discussions so far and to tie up a few loose ends. The various chapters of this book have attempted to uncover the various issues that need to be addressed in examining the biblical material on women. It is now time to bring the various aspects together to present the case in favour of women being allowed equal opportunity to men in serving the purposes of God.

1. Summary of this book

If we understand God-given authority to be delegated and that those who are appointed to leadership must make themselves accountable to God, then many of the emotive questions surrounding a woman having authority disappear. True authority must be Christ-like and is given so that the person in authority can serve others. It should not be used to self-promote nor to dominate over others. True authority is to release others, not to demand that the will of the leader is done. Given this understanding the issue facing us is whether or not a woman can have authority to lay down her life in emulation of Christ. As we have seen there should be no objection to this. (Chapter 1.)

The only aspect where a woman is to submit in a specific sense (given that mutual submission is commanded of all believers) is within the marriage relationship — the Bible does not teach that all women must submit to all men. However even the marriage relationship is not one where the husband can dictate — rather he is called to release his wife to her future in God. Further, there is a case to be made that to understand the marriage relationship in very strict terms would be to fail to grasp the nature of the household codes as outlined by Paul. There are occasions when Paul advocates that compromise is the best way forward, for the sake of the gospel, so there is scope for the married couple to explore different models of marriage. The parameters set should be one where neither party is in a dictatorship position and the husband understands that his first calling is to the marriage and any family that the couple have. The goal of the marriage relationship should be of 'one flesh' agreement to work together to fulfil the will and call of God. (This is explored in Chapter 4.)

Our ecclesiology (understanding of church) undoubtedly can shape our conclusions on the subject of women. The means by which leadership is recognised differs within the different traditions and if our tradition is from the more pneumatic wing of the church there should be less difficulty in accepting women in leadership positions — the overriding issue within that tradition being the requirement that we discover whom God has anointed. Even within the other traditions this aspect of the anointing of the Spirit should not be neglected but must challenge how we respond. (Chapter 2.)

A large part of the debate will still centre around the Bible and its teaching. This is why a large part of the book focused directly on the biblical record of women and their role (Chapter 3), hermeneutical issues (Chapter 5) and the seemingly restrictive passages (Chapter 6). I am sure that not all will have been convinced by the conclusions I have reached but my appeal is that those who take a different approach do not accuse those who, like myself, see no restriction placed on women, of disrespecting the authority of Scripture. It is not a respect for the authority of Scripture but our understanding of what it teaches that is in question.

In all the discussions on Scripture I want to affirm the authority of Scripture. Letty M. Russell makes a balanced response which I would wholeheartedly endorse:

> The Bible has authority in my life because it makes sense of my experience and speaks to me about meaning and purpose of my humanity in Jesus Christ. In spite of its ancient and patriarchal worldviews, in spite of its inconsistencies and mixed messages, the story of the God's love affair with the world leads me to a

vision of New Creation that implies my life... [Its] authority in my life stems from its story of God's invitation to participate in the restoration of wholeness, peace, and justice in the world.[1]

In conclusion then I have sought to address the following issues: the nature of authority, ecclesiology, missiology and hermeneutics; all of which has been implicitly shaped by an eschatological theology that there is a new humanity that is in Christ. For those who disagree with my conclusions they too need to address these same issues. It is not sufficient to quote Scripture, and the most significant aspect that would need to be established, in my opinion, would be on the nature of the eschatological redemption that Christ has purchased. The new creation that Christ has inaugurated is not simply a restoration of the original creation; in Christ all things have become new.[2] Kevin Giles puts this succinctly in a recent article stating that 'Eden cannot give the ideal because there the devil was active and sin was possible. The church as the eschatological people of God is always to look forward, and seek to realise in its corporate life the perfection to be known in the new heaven and the new earth, where all inequalities will be abolished.'[3]

2. Does God use a woman when he cannot find a man?

This argument has been used to explain the 'exceptions' in Scripture. However it needs to be exposed for the deception that it is. Although

---

[1]Quoted in *Women & Men: Gender in the Church*, (ed.) Carol Penner (Scottdale / Waterloo: Herald, 1998), p. 29.
[2]See Ephes. 2:15 for the one new humanity that Christ has redeemed; Gal. 6:15 for the new creation realities. All of which are possible because through the resurrection Jesus became the Last Adam, or eschatological human (1 Cor. 15:45). To translate the transformation that takes place for those who are in Christ as simply they become a 'new creation / creature' (2 Cor. 5:17) is far too limiting. The sense is much more of 'for those who are in Christ, [they enter] a new creation, everything old has gone, look the new realities have come'.
[3]Kevin Giles, 'A Critique of the 'Novel' Contemporary Interpretation of 1 Timothy 2:9-15 Given in the Book, *Women in the Church*. Part II', *The Evangelical Quarterly*, Vol. LXXII, No 3 (July, 2000), p. 199.

there is a proverb that says 'the exception proves the rule', we must insist that the exception cannot prove the truth, for truth is unchanging and does not have exceptions. Women in leadership cannot end up as the exception which proves the rule. Either it is wrong for them to be in leadership, or we have established a rule which is false. So we cannot claim that God simply uses a woman when he cannot find a man, and use this as sufficient explanation for some women being involved in ministry.

In fact this claim, that God only uses a woman when he cannot find a man, has even more serious implications. In her book *Equal to Serve*, Hull deals with this by saying that, if it is wrong for God to use a woman, then it is wrong under any circumstances. Otherwise a church leadership, in the light of the fact that they had insufficient funds to finance their church programme, could say that they planned to use stolen money. If it is wrong by God's decree, then it is wrong and the ends cannot justify the means.

This sort of question raises the dilemma which many people find themselves in. They recognise that God has gifted women in a specific area and that they could use those gifts to fulfil a role of ministry or leadership. If those roles are not open to them, then it begs the question of why God gifted them in this way in the first place.

3.   Men and women working together

Once we have established a theological basis for the release of women into leadership, we face the practical issues of men and women working together. There are dangers involved when women take their place alongside men. There is the very real danger of sexual temptation and sin, and to avoid this certain safeguards need to be put in place. Everyone needs other people around them to whom they can be accountable and I suggest that we ensure there are people around us whom we trust who know us intimately, which must include the vulnerable areas, and can watch our backs. I hope it goes without saying but those people need to be our partners, if married, and those of the same gender if the vulnerability is in the sexual area.

However it is not simply in the obvious area of sexual temptation that the challenges arise. Many male-only groups relate in a certain way and if they are to see women included in on those groups the way they relate together must change. This is normally a challenge to the men (and normally a challenge to be more open, honest and intimate with one another) but is very necessary as those women will enable any group to be more Christ-like in behaviour. So leadership styles need to be examined.

A third challenge is which women should be included. Often times an assumption is made that the women should be the wives of leaders. This raises a number of questions: what about the singles whom Paul indicated were better placed to serve God without distraction? Are all wives of leaders called into leadership?[4] If husband and wives have always to work together I believe we will institute a limiting model for the future (this is not to deny that God has placed husbands and wives together and their individual callings impact on their partner). I am not stipulating how we should respond — I am simply saying that we need to be clear on what basis wives (or husbands) are included on any leadership team.

Working together at any level is a challenge, and the mixing of the genders presents us with greater challenges. But here again is the opportunity, within safe parameters, to demonstrate that it is the gospel of Jesus Christ that sets us free to be truly ourselves, and enables us to set others free. There is a great need to see a body of people who are relating together as brothers and sisters not on the basis of sexual attraction or reaction.

---

[4]We will also have to face the wonderfully challenging aspect of whether all husbands of female leaders are called into leadership.

4. Should the church follow the world?

An accusation that is sometimes aimed at those who take a similar position to myself is that there is something intrinsically wrong when the church follows the world. The rise of feminism began in the world, it is argued, and the desire for equality within the church indicates that the church has followed the world's lead. This accusation raises a number of issues, two of which are: does God always initiate something new in the church? And has the church actually followed the world in its approach?

How we respond to the first question relates to our view of the Spirit's activity. If we have a developed view of the Spirit at work in creation we can accommodate the possibility that many expressions of justice are in fact reflective of the Spirit's cry.[5] If God's rule extends to history and the world, there should be little difficulty in accepting the possibility that diverse movements can be partly inspired by a divine agenda. This does not mean that every aspect of those movements need be endorsed.

The second issue I raised, needs more careful examining. My own perspective is that the issue of freedom for women was raised primarily within a non-church context, but that Christians who responded sought to hear the voice of the Spirit, and then test that voice against the teachings of Jesus. Hence they might have been provoked to re-examine the biblical material through the secular feminist agenda, but in the final analysis this only caused them to ask the question as to how faithfully they themselves were following the Christ they professed to know. So the world can provoke, for God is at work in the world by his Spirit, but the church must then undertake to follow Christ regardless of the cost.

---

[5]The material in Clark Pinnock's work on the Holy Spirit, *Flame of Love* (Downers Grove: IVP, 1997) on the Spirit's activity in creation is most informative.

5.   A call to commitment

My final plea is not that my discussions are agreed with, but that we learn how to live together as the community of Jesus, regardless of our social, racial or gender differences. With regard to our subject in hand: we must purpose to work for the release of women and all other previously 'absent' people groups. It is for such a time as this that God has called each and everyone of us to the kingdom — that kingdom we pray for to be expressed on earth. Let us decide to lay the minimum of restriction on one another and see the maximum amount of release. There is a world waiting to see our liberty — not the freedom to sin, but the freedom to exercise godly authority as we lay down our lives for one another and for the world that Jesus loved.

Let me leave you with a gentle, but clear, feminine voice: 'Just as we can no longer justify slavery, we can no longer justify the suppression of women's voices who are helping us along the path of Christian discipleship and obedience.'[6]

---

[6]Adelia Neufeld Wiens, 'Gender in the New Testament', in *Women & Men: Gender in the Church*, (ed.) Carol Penner (Scottdale / Waterloo: Herald Press, 1998), p. 29.

APPENDICES

Two appendices follow: the first one simply makes reference to material quoted in *Men & Women: Gender in the Church* edited by Carol Penner) which I have been unable to substantiate as I came across the material too late to interact with at any meaningful level. However, I thought it was of sufficient interest and that it could serve readers of this book who might have time to follow it through with their own research. The main appendix, which immediately follows this introduction, is a reproduction of a paper by Sheri R. Benvenuti in which she addresses the issue of the release of women within Pentecostalism. Generally speaking within movements that claim to be Spirit-inspired women are given roles that were previously considered to be inappropriate for them. I have already referred to Chris Cartwright's paper in chapter 2, where he indicates the historic situation covering ordination within the Elim Pentecostal Movement. The Elim movement has its roots in the Pentecostal revival that took place in Los Angeles on Azusa Street and the leadership of that revival included women (as well as crossing racial barriers). From Azusa Street a magazine was produced entitled, *The Apostolic Faith,* and two quotes from it will indicate that they understood the outpouring of the Spirit to have challenged gender inequality:

> Before Jesus ascended to heaven, holy anointing oil had never been poured on a woman's head; but before He organized His church, He called them all into the upper room, both men and women, and anointed them with the oil of the Holy Ghost, thus qualifying them all to minister in this Gospel. On the day of Pentecost they all preached through the power of the Holy Ghost. In Christ Jesus there is neither male nor female, all are one.

It is contrary to the Scriptures that women should not have her part in the salvation work to which God has called her... It is the same Holy Spirit in the woman as in the man.[1]

Cheryl Bridges Johns explained the freedom for women in early Pentecostalism as fuelled by 'an eschatological urgency and equality in which the Spirit enlisted everyone for the mission at hand.'[2] The urgency dictated that no-one was excluded from the call to proclaim and the anointing of the Spirit was given without distinction.

Rather than continue to document historic situations I have reproduced this paper which was delivered to the Pentecostal Charismatic Churches of North America at 1996 Memphis Miracle Revisited. It was entitled, 'Pentecostal Women in Ministry: Where Do We Go From Here?' No adjustments to the text have been made: the only adjustments are where some of the formatting has been changed. It is reproduced with the author's permission.

---

[1] The first quote is from the September 1907 edition, p. 3; the second from the January 1908 edition, p. 2. Both quotes appear in Dale T. Irvin 'Drawing All Together in One Bond of Love: The Ecumenical Vision of William J. Seymour and the Azusa Street Revival', *Journal of Pentecostal Theology*, Issue 6 (April, 1995), p. 47. Irvin also notes that there were some discussions on feminine gendered imagery for the Holy Spirit as early as 1907.

[2] 'Pentecostal Spirituality and Women' in Harold Hunter & Peter Hocken (eds.) *All Together in One Place*, (Sheffield: SAP, 1993), p. 162.

Appendix 1

Pentecostal Women in Ministry: Where Do We Go From Here?

By Sheri R. Benvenuti

Pentecostal women who are called to ministry walk a fine and often precarious line. We, on the one hand, are not radical feminists who demand certain fights, suspicion patriarchal hierarchy as the greatest of all human evils, or refer to God as "she" at every turn. However, on the other hand, we are not simply passive about our call to ministry. We do notice the "man's world" in which we must function, and we understand that the "female," too, helps make up what we know about the image of God. We are not women who wish to displace men, nor do we view women who are not called to ministry as being in any way inferior. We are women who simply and humbly ask that we be given room to be obedient to the Lord who has called us. We are certainly not the first generation of Pentecostal women who have pursued such an opportunity.

When one reads about some of the great women in our history such as Aimee Semple McPherson, Alice Belle Garrigus, Maria Woodworth-Etter, Marie Burgess, Kathryn Kuhlman, and Mae Eleanore Frey, it is encouraging to know that these extremely gifted women ministered with great success at a time in history that did not make life easy for them. Their call to preach seemed to supersede everything else in their lives, motivating them to pay a difficult price to fulfill God's will. Their faithfulness is of great encouragement to every Pentecostal woman in ministry today.

However, there is some disappointment at the present state of women in ministry in our Pentecostal fellowships. While there are indications that a few of our denominations are experiencing a small increase in the total amount of women who serve in those fellowships[1], the figures reveal that there will be a slow upward climb ahead for women who are called to serve.   I must confess that I have a vested interest in the issue of women in ministry, not only from an academic perspective, but also from a personal point of view. I have been a Pentecostal minister for the last twenty-five years. During this time the discussion of Pentecostal women in ministry has come to the point where much work has been done both biblically and historically to redefine the opportunity for women in ministry positions. However, my experience still causes me to resonate with the great Assemblies of God evangelist, Mae Eleanore Frey who once said, "... for God-fearing, intelligent, Spirit-filled women, upon whom God has set his seal in their ministry, to have to sit and listen to men haggle over the matter of their place in the ministry is humiliating to say the least."[2] In addition to this difficult personal situation for women, there is also the greater reality of a world desperately needing every anointed person to preach the gospel, while the Church busies itself with unending doctrinal debate over who is qualified to minister in what position. We are, in a sense, watching the house burn down while arguing about which fire truck to use. The time has come for Pentecostal women in ministry to leave the arena of debate and simply be who they are and do what God has called them to do.

In view of the need for practical solutions which will work to encourage women in this endeavor, the historical context from which we

---

[1]For specific statistics on two Pentecostal fellowships, the Assemblies of God, and the Church of God, refer to 'The Contemporary, State of Women in Ministry in the Assemblies of God' by Deborah M. Gill, and 'Perfect Liberty to Preach the Gospel: Women Ministers in the Church of God' by David Roebuck in *Pneuma: The Journal of the Society for Pentecostal Studies* 17/1 (Spring 1995), pp. 25-36.
[2]Mae Eleanor Frey, 'Selected Letters of Mae Eleanore Frey', Comp. by Edith L. Blumhofer, *Pneuma* 17/1 (Spring 1995), p. 78.

function is vitally important for Pentecostal women in ministry simply because it not only sets precedent for what we do, but also because history has a way of teaching some invaluable practical lessons. With this in view, there are at least three important needs that can be identified to justify a place for Pentecostal women in ministry.

The Need for Pentecostals to Return to Their Roots

The moment this statement is made, one must assume that Pentecostals have indeed strayed from their initial identity. The fact that the participation of women in ministry is even an issue within the context of Pentecostalism suggests this to be true. There are at least two things which have contributed to this change from the early days of Pentecostalism.

First, as Pentecostal denominations began to formalize their structure, women who were active in every type of ministry position were simply left out of denominational leadership roles. Up to this point, in fact, there is little to suggest that women doing the work of the ministry, holding positions as pastors, teachers, and evangelists, were even questioned in the validity of their function. Men and women of that day seemed to be grounded in the understanding that because God chose women to participate in the New Testament Holy Spirit baptism experience, it was only logical that they, too, should carry the message of the gospel. In the words of Mae Eleanore Frey, "God Almighty is no fool — I say it with all reverence — Would He fill a woman with the Holy Ghost — endow her with ability — give her a vision of souls and then tell her to shut her mouth?"[3]

In their insightful article concerning this idea, Charles H. Barfoot and Gerald T. Sheppard hold that in those early days, three factors were responsible for the equality of the sexes in Pentecostal ministry:

---

[3]Ibid., p. 77.

For Such A Time As This

1. The importance of "a calling."

2. The confirmation of the call through the recognition of the presence of ministry gifting in the person by the community.

3. The community's eschatological belief that they were experiencing the "latter rain" in which "your sons and your daughters will prophesy."[4]

Barfoot and Sheppard suggest, however, that "as routinization and regimentation of community relationships set in, reactions did occur against the [Pentecostal] movement's prophesying daughters."[5] One vital reaction to which Barfoot and Sheppard refer involves the whole question of authority. That is, should women in ministry have positions of authority over men? As Pentecostal fellowships moved from the pioneer phase of their development into the formalization of church structure, a shift began to take place in the minds of the early framers of these groups. Where once women were free to function in any ministry gift, now some were unable to fulfill their call by being relegated to newly defined "feminine" roles, while others paid a great price to remain true to their call. That the idea of authority should be at the center of the discussion not only determined the path that early Pentecostalism was to take, but was a direct reversal of the position taken by the early pioneers of the movement.

In early Pentecostalism, authority was never the issue; rather, servanthood was always the focal point of one's ministry calling. Even the manner in which the church services were conducted suggested that early Pentecostals fully believed that the Holy Spirit himself held absolute authority, and the Spirit anointed whomever he chose to serve the body of believers. Frank Bartleman describes those early days:

---

[4]Charles H. Barfoot and Gerald T. Sheppard, 'Prophetic Vs. Priestly Religion: The Changing Role of Women Clergy in Classical Pentecostal Churches', *Review of Religious Research* 22/1 (September), p. 4.
[5]Ibid., p. 4.

Brother Seymour was recognized as the nominal leader in charge. But we had no pope or hierarchy... The Lord Himself was leading... We did not honor men for their advantage, in means or education, but rather for their God-given 'gifts...' The Lord was liable to burst through any one. We prayed for this continually. Someone would finally get up anointed for the message. All seemed to recognize this and gave way. It might be a child, a woman, or a man.[6]

While deconstruction of structural organization is not what is called for, what is necessary is a return to the biblical, and early Pentecostal, understanding that all authority is defined by the degree to which one serves. That is to say, for the Pentecostal, authority is not derived through position alone, as some may assert, but rather is found in the individual who serves the body of Christ through the power of the Holy Spirit. With this understanding, the gender of the individual in question becomes irrelevant, for no one ever debates which gender is qualified to serve.

The second contributing factor is what Cecil Robeck calls "the 'evangelicalization' of Pentecostals."[7]

While Pentecostals have achieved a sense of acceptance and respectability through their relationship with the National Association of Evangelicals, 'as evangelical values have been adopted by Pentecostals, the role of women in ministry has suffered.'[8] Pentecostal denominations have traditionally allowed women much greater freedom in ministry roles than their evangelical counterparts. A return to our Pentecostal roots, in this case, would mean a return to the theology and experience that make

---

[6]Frank Bartleman, *What Really Happened on "Azusa Street"?* (Northridge, California: Voice Christian Publications, 1966), pp. 32-34.
[7]Cecil M. Robeck, Jr., 'National Association of Evangelicals', in *Dictionary of Pentecostal and Charismatic Movements*, Stanley M. Burgess and Gary B. McGee, eds. (Grand Rapids: Zondervan, 1988), p. 635.
[8]Ibid., p. 635.

us who we are: a diverse, yet unified group of individuals who are each empowered by the Holy Spirit to function in ministry gifts.

Each of the women who were involved in ministry in the early days were women who were incredibly and undeniably gifted. These were women who reaped a great harvest. Many people were converted, many were healed, denominational boundaries were broken, and men, women, and children received the outpouring of their own personal Pentecost. Edith Blumhofer asserts that:

> In the early Pentecostal movement, having the "anointing" was far more important than one's sex. As evangelistic bands carried the full gospel across the country, women who were recognized as having the anointing of the Holy Spirit shared with men in the preaching ministry... A person's call — and how other believers viewed it — was far more important than [ministerial credentials].[9]

For a Pentecostal, one's call to ministry is confirmed by the gifting. While denominational ordination is an important factor in validating one's call, it is simply that, a validation of the ministry one is already doing through the empowerment of the Holy Spirit.[10] Consequently, women in ministry who are Pentecostals should be just that, Pentecostals. They should be encouraged to pray for the sick, preach, teach, evangelize, and do the work of the ministry, understanding that their validation comes through the gifting of the Spirit, as well as the corresponding ordination of the Church.

---

[9]Edith Blumhofer, *The Assemblies of God: A Popular History* (Springfield: Gospel Publishing House, 1985), p. 137.
[10]Refer to the ordination of Paul and Barnabas in Acts 13. Both men were already leaders in the church at Antioch when 'the Holy Spirit said, 'Set apart for me Barnabas and Saul for the work to which I have called them'.'

The Need for Role Models

There is no greater example of the necessity for women to have role models than that found in the life and ministry of Aimee Semple McPherson. After 10 years of grueling evangelistic work, McPherson decided to settle down in Los Angeles in 1921. She purchased property near Echo Park, designed and built Angelus Temple, dedicating the new building on January 1, 1923. By the time she was thirty-three years old, Aimee Semple McPherson had established the first Christian radio station in the United States, a 5,300 seat auditorium in which thousands of people were saved and healed, a Bible College, and ultimately a denomination, all of which are still in operation today.[11] The International Church of the Foursquare Gospel now has well over 1.9 million members, with over 31,000 churches and meeting places in 72 countries around the world.[12]

While McPherson was uniquely gifted and greatly used of God, she did not exist in a vacuum. Other influential women had begun to pave the way for her, providing many models to follow and, as a result, a certain level of acceptance for women in ministry that she otherwise may not have enjoyed. The number of women providing a legacy of leadership in the Pentecostal movement were numerous. In addition to those women addressed in the articles under consideration, there were others such as Maria Woodworth-Etter, who by the end of 1885, was drawing an estimated 25,000 people to her camp meetings. Also active in the Movement was Marie Burgess, who after having been baptized with the Holy Spirit in 1906 under the ministry of Charles Parham, began preaching in Illinois, Ohio, and Michigan, eventually founding the great Glad Tidings Hall in New York.

McPherson herself was not unaware of the impact she would have upon women in ministry, and in fact encouraged other women to

---

[11]Rolf K. McPherson Interview, San Dimas, CA. October, 1992.
[12]1995 Ministry Report, International Church of the Foursquare Gospel.

follow her lead. In a lecture to one of her Bible School classes, she stated:

> This is the only church, I am told, that is ordaining women preachers. Even the Pentecostal works, in some cases, have said, "no women preachers." But I am opening the door, and as long as Sister McPherson is alive, she is going to hold the door open and say, "Ladies, come!"[13]

She was evidently true to her word, for by 1944, the year of her death, women accounted for 67% of the ordained clergy in the denomination which she founded, the International Church of the Foursquare Gospel. Following her death, however, a change in the number of ordained women began to occur. By the late seventies, the figure had dropped to 42%.[14] By 1993, the number of ordained women had decreased to approximately 38%[15] While this ratio is relatively high compared to other Pentecostal denominations, it must be noted that a great percentage of these ordained women are wives of ordained pastors who do not necessarily function in legitimate church leadership roles, with only a handful of these women functioning as senior pastors of a congregation.

Even more interesting is the lack of women found within corporate leadership in the denomination. Because all executive offices are appointed, using senior pastors as the pool of possible candidates, coupled with the fact that there are few female senior pastors in the denomination, of the 34 executive council members, only 5 are women, with two of these women serving in traditionally female roles as Assistant Secretary and Director of Women's Ministries. Further, of the 166 divisional representatives, none are female.[16] While there may be other

---

[13]Class Notes on the Book of Acts, LIFE Bible College, Los Angeles, N/D.
[14]Barfoot and Sheppard, p. 15.
[15]1993 Ministry Report, International Church of the Foursquare Gospel.
[16]1993 Ministry Report, International Church of the Foursquare Gospel.

contributing factors, the lack of women in high-profile positions has surely made a strong contribution to the decrease of women who hold senior ministry positions within the Foursquare Church. Could it be that the absence of a powerful example such as Aimee Semple McPherson has contributed to this decline?

This phenomenon has not gone unnoticed by some of the leaders in the denomination. In fact, in February of 1995, the International Church sponsored the first National Women's Leadership Conference in Fort Worth, Texas. The 900 women who were in attendance strongly responded to the theme of the conference: Catch the Vision: Create a Legacy. These women obviously believe that it is not only important for Pentecostal women in ministry to fulfill their call in the present, but that by doing so, they will also create greater opportunity for future female leadership as well by modeling Spirit empowered ministry to the next generation of women.

The Need for Affirmation

Pentecostal women who are called to ministry have need of affirmation from three specific sources. Harvey Cox, in his Fire From on High, has noticed the high value Pentecostals have put on "direct revelation." In his chapter that concerns Pentecostal women in ministry, Cox says of a testimony he heard:

> It went a long way in answering my question about how so many women win the right to preach in a church which, at least technically, forbids it. It clearly demonstrated why Pentecostals, who take the authority of the Bible very seriously but also believe in direct revelation through visions, have opened a wider space for women than most other Christian denominations have.

What the Bible says is one thing, but when God speaks to you directly, that supersedes everything else.[17]

While it is true that Pentecostal women in ministry have had a tendency to base the validity of their ministry on the "call" experience alone, one must consider that the call itself requires scriptural basis. Women must first function in ministry with the validity of their call resting in scripture, not in spite of it. Pentecostals must hold to the truth that gender bias runs in direct opposition to the entire message of the gospel. While it is true that in the old fallen order, sex discrimination is practiced, redemption in Christ has set us free from the practice of using gender as the criteria for determining positions of leadership within the Church. Paul declares that "there is neither Jew nor Greek, slave nor free, male nor female, for you are all one in Christ Jesus" (Gal. 3:28). Paul declares this rather radical statement within the context of a discussion with the Galatians concerning the futility of their attempts to satisfy the Old Testament law (particularly circumcision) by their own works, while continuing to maintain that they are living by grace. In Paul's view, circumcision, specifically a male rite, had fulfilled its purpose in the Old Testament. In the New Testament, however, the old rite has been replaced by the rite of baptism, in which all believers — male and female, slave and free, Jew or Greek — can participate. Stanley Grenz says of this passage in Galatians that,

> Paul indicates that the transition from circumcision to baptism has destroyed the significance of the distinctions between persons which formerly were used to establish social hierarchies. These include appeals not only to ethnic heritage (Jew and Gentile) and social status (free and slave) but also to gender

---

[17]Harvey Cox, *Fire From Heaven: The Rise of Pentecostal Spirituality and the Reshaping of Religion in The Twenty-first Century* (Reading, Massachusetts: Addison-Wesley Publishing Company, 1995) p. 131.

differentiations (male and female). Therefore the hierarchy of male over female introduced by the Fall is now outmoded ... [18]

For Pentecostals to live according to any hierarchical structure which exalts one race, one social group, or one gender over another is to bring ourselves under a bondage that was never purposed for us in Christ. That is not to say that organization is not necessary, it certainly is. However, we must live according to the New Testament injunction to "be subject to one another out of reverence for Christ" (Eph. 5:21). All human relationship within the context of the community of God must always be guided by equal submission.

Further, looking to scripture as the foundation for ministry means that the "problem passages" must be wrestled through, using all of the academic tools available. My personal experience has been that once these issues were dealt with, in a manner true to hermeneutical principles that provided solid answers, I felt a confidence in my ministry that had not been experienced up to this point. In addition, not only is it important for the Pentecostal female minister for her own benefit to understand that she is functioning in ministry because of a scriptural foundation (not in spite of it), this knowledge will also serve to neutralize opposing doctrine, thereby opening a greater opportunity for women in official ministry positions.

Secondly, women are entering Bible Colleges and Seminaries in staggering numbers. In fact, according to 1993 statistics, 25-30 percent of the students enrolled in seminary degree programs in the United States are women.[19] Clearly, women are sensing the call of God to full-time ministry; as a result, they are responding to their call by pursuing formal education. It is vital, then, that our Pentecostal colleges offer

---

[18]Stanley J. Grenz and Denise Muir Kjesbo, *Women in the Church: A Biblical Theology of Women in Ministry* (Downers Grove: InterVarsity Press, 1995), p. 178.
[19]Gordon A. Wetmore, 'God-Called Women', *The Seminary Tower* 49/1 (Fall 1993.) p. 1.

education concerning women in leadership within the context of the Pentecostal distinctive. However, this education must not be in any way limited to women or to the subject of women in leadership, but should encompass both historical and Biblical analysis arising from a Pentecostal tradition. In short, young Pentecostals need to be taught the distinctives of their Pentecostal heritage and identity, which include the scriptural validation of ministry for women. This effort will not only give female students great confidence in their call through proper understanding and equipping, but will also serve to inform our young male Pentecostals, as well, preparing them to deal with the reality of the female ministers they will surely encounter in their ministries.

Last, the call of God, in addition to the act of ordination for female Pentecostals, becomes a moot issue unless ministry opportunities are available to women. Today, I can not look across my desk at a young female who is about to graduate with a degree in Pastoral Ministry and confidently say to her that there will be a position open to her in the local church for which she has been called and trained. For example, in the Assemblies of God in 1993, 15.2% of credentialed ministers were females, but 40.2% of that number were 65 years or older. And, only 1.06% of all credentialed ministers were female senior pastors. Further, there are some Pentecostal denominations that do not yet allow women full ordination. Because women who are called to ministry cannot be disobedient to the will of God for their lives and must be true to their calling, this lack of opportunity within the Pentecostal ranks will, I fear, cause many of our brightest and best ministers to defect to non-Pentecostal denominations where their fire and zeal is most welcomed, regardless of their gender.

Therefore, our Pentecostal fellowships must be willing to give equal opportunity to those women who are called to ministry, not merely allowing them the more traditional female roles in the church, but recognizing the possibility that no position in church/servant leadership is gender restricted.

Conclusion

Today, Pentecostals find themselves asking what it means to be truly Pentecostal. With a new appreciation for education rising within their ranks, young Pentecostals, both male and female, are beginning to notice that in the early days of the Movement, Pentecostals were involved in the women's suffrage movement, were conscientious objectors, and were vitally involved in many areas of social reform. Further, there are some who are now calling for an abandonment of much of the evangelical theology which is diametrically opposed to the original Pentecostal experience, while at the same time holding to a form of biblical literalism, which is in effect, having the result of the development of a Pentecostal hermeneutic which is more in line with the Pentecostal experience.

Ideally, as women become more assured in their calling to ministry, more confident in their gifting by the Holy Spirit, and are affirmed in who they are biblically and historically through the process of education and ministry opportunity in their fellowship, these women will rise to the occasion.

> "If..women are [no] less capable than men of piety, zeal, learning and whatever else seems necessary for the [ministry], then why ... should the church not draw on the huge reserves which could pour into the priesthood if women were here, as in so many professions, put on the same footing with men?"[20]

Why, indeed?

---

[20]Paul K. Jewett, *The Ordination of Women* (Grand Rapids: Wm. B. Eerdmans Publishing Co., 1980), p. 14.

Appendix 2

The following are simply two quotes from Men & Women: Gender in the Church:

> A paper soon to be published by Harvard Divinity School cites a fifth-century papal letter that orders bishops to stop ordaining women as priests, and a ninth-century Italian bishop who stated that women shared the priestly ministry equally with men.[1]

A blatant example of altering historical records may be seen in the defacing of a mosaic in a Roman church, dating from about the fifth century. It depicts the head of a veiled women with the title of episcopa (overseer, bishop) written over it. The woman's name Theodo[ra] was written vertically beside the figure. But the last two letters that make the name feminine had been removed from the mosaic and replaced by pieces from a later period, leaving the masculine name, Theodo.[2]

---

[1]P. 146 citing Paul Smith Is it OK to Call God Mother? (Peabody: Hendrickson, 1993), p. 113.

[2]P. 146, citing Margaret E. Howe, Women and Church Leadership (Grand Rapids: Zondervan, 1982), pp. 36-38.

Bibliography

Anderson, J. A., 'Women's Warfare and Ministry', *Christian Herald* (London, 1935)

Arnold, Clinton, *Powers of Darkness* (Downers Grove: IVP; Leicester: IVP, 1992)

Atkins, Anne, *Split Image* (London: Hodder & Stoughton, 1987)

Barnett, Paul W., 'Wives and Women's Ministry (1 Timothy 2:11-15)', *Evangelical Quarterly*, Vol. LXI, No. 3 (July, 1989)

Benvenuti, Sheri, 'Releasing Women in Ministry', paper accessed at the web site, [http://www.pctii.org/cyber1.html]

Birney, Leroy, 'The Role of Women in the New Testament Church', *Christian Brethren Review Journal*, No. 33 (December 1982)

Black, Hugh B., *A Trumpet call to Women* (Greenock: New Dawn Books, 1988)

Branick, Vincent, *The House Church in the Writings of St. Paul* (Wilmington, DE: Michael Glazier, 1989)

Brauch, Manfred, *Hard Sayings of Paul* (London: Hodder & Stoughton, 1990)

Bruce, F. F., *The Book of Acts*, NICNT (Grand Rapids: Eerdmans, 1954)

———— *The Epistle to the Galatians*, NIGTC (Exeter: Paternoster, 1982)

Clark, Stephen B., *Man and Woman in Christ* (Ann Arbor, MI: Servant Books, 1980)

Cox, Harvey, *Fire from Heaven* (Reading, MA: Addison-Wesley, 1994)

Cartwright, Chris, 'The Role of Women in the Government of the Church', unpublished paper

Cotterell, Peter and Max Turner, *Linguistics and Biblical Interpretation* (London: SPCK, 1989)

Daly, Mary, *The Church and the Second Sex* (New York: Harper & Row, 1968)

Dunn, James, *Romans 9-16*, Word commentary series (Waco, TX: Word, 1991)

———— *The Theology of Paul the Apostle*, (Grand Rapids / Cambridge: Eerdmans, 1998)

———— *The Theology of Paul's Letter to the Galatians*, (Cambridge: CUP, 1993)

Durnbaugh, Donald, *The Believers' Church* (New York: Macmillan, 1968 / Scottdale: Herald, 1985)

Elliott, Neil, *Liberating Paul* (New York: Orbis, 1994; Sheffield: Sheffield Academic Press, 1995)

Ellis, E. Earle, *Pauline Theology — Ministry and Society* (Grand Rapids: Eerdmans; Exeter: Paternoster, 1989)

Evans, Mary, *Woman in the Bible* (Exeter: Paternoster, 1983)

Fahrer, Wally, *Building on the Rock* (Scottdale: Herald, 1995)

Fee, Gordon, *1 and 2 Timothy, Titus*, NIBC series (Peabody: Hendrickson, 1988; Carlisle: Paternoster, 1995)

———— *The First Epistle to the Corinthians*, NICNT series (Grand Rapids: Eerdmans, 1987)

Finger, Thomas, *Christian Theology*, Vol. 2 (Scottdale, Herald, 1989)

Gasque, W. Ward & Laurel Gasque, 'F. F. Bruce: A Mind for what Matters', *Christianity Today* (April 7, 1989)

Giles, Kevin, 'The Biblical Argument for Slavery: Can the Bible Mislead', *Evangelical Quarterly*, Vol. LXVI, No. 1 (January, 1994)

————— 'A Critique of the 'Novel' Contemporary Interpretation of 1 Timothy 2:9-15 Given in the Book, *Women in the Church*. Part II', *The Evangelical Quarterly*, Vol. LXXII, No 3 (July, 2000)

Guitiérrez, Gustavo, *A Theology of Liberation* (London: SCM, 1988)

Grenz, Stanley, *Theology for the Community of God* (Carlisle: Paternoster, 1994)

Grudem, Wayne & John Piper (eds.), *Recovering Biblical Manhood and Womanhood: A Response to Biblical Feminism* (Wheaton: Crossway, 1991)

Hamerton-Kelly, Robert, *God the Father: Theology and Patriarchy in the Teaching of Jesus* (Philadelphia: Fortress, 1979)

Hansen, G. Walter, *Galatians*, IVP NT commentary series (Downers Grove / Leicester: IVP, 1994)

Hull, Gretchen Gaebelein, *Equal to Serve* (London: Scripture Union, 1989)

Hurley, James, *Man and Woman in Biblical Perspective* (London: IVP, 1981)

Hyatt, Eddie, *2000 Years of Charismatic Christianity* (Tulsa / Chicota: Hyatt International Ministries, 1996)

Irvin, Dale T., 'Drawing All Together in One Bond of Love: The Ecumenical Vision of William J. Seymour and the Azusa Street Revival', *Journal of Pentecostal Theology*, Issue 6 (April, 1995)

Jewett, Paul, *Man as Male and Female* (Grand Rapids: Eerdmans, 1975)

Johns, Cheryl Bridges, 'Pentecostal Spirituality and the Conscientization of Women', in Harold Hunter & Peter Hocken (eds.) *All Together in One Place: Theological Papers from the Brighton Conference on World Evangelization*, Journal of Pentecostal Theology Supplement 4 (Sheffield: SAP, 1993)

Keener, Craig, *And Marries Another...* (Peabody: Hendrickson, 1991)

———— *Paul, Women and Wives* (Peabody: Hendrickson, 1992)

Krauss, C. Norman, *God our Savior* (Scottdale: Herald, 1991)

Kroeger, Richard Clark & Catherine Clark Kroeger, *I Suffer Not a Woman, Rethinking 1 Timothy 2:11-15 in Light of Ancient Evidence* (Grand Rapids: Baker, 1992)

Laughery, G. J., 'Paul: Anti-marriage? Anti-sex? Ascetic? A Dialogue with 1 Corinthians 7:1-40', *Evangelical Quarterly*, Vol. LXIX, No. 2 (April, 1997)

Leonard, Christine, *A Giant in Ghana* (Chichester: New Wine, 1989)

Marshall, Tom, *Understanding Leadership* (Chichester: Sovereign World, 1991)

McCallum, Dennis and Gary DeLashmutt, 'Men, Women and Gender Roles in Marriage', paper published at the Web site [http://www.xenos.org/ books/mythmw.htm]

McClendon Jr., James, *Systematic Theology*, Vol. 2 (Nashville: Abingdon, 1994)

Mickelsen, Alvera (ed.), *Women, Authority & The Bible* (Downers Grove: IVP, 1986)

Moltmann, Jürgen, 'A Pentecostal Theology of Life' *Journal of Pentecostal Theology*, Issue 9, (Sheffield: SAP, October 1996)

Morris, Leon, *The Gospel according to John*, NICNT (Grand Rapids: Eerdmans, 1971)

Newbigin, Lesslie, *The Household of God* (London: SCM, 1953 / New York: Friendship, 1954)

Noble, Christine, *What in the world is God saying about Women* (Eastbourne: Kingsway 1990)

O'Brien, P. T., 'Church' in Hawthorne, Gerald, Ralph Martin and Daniel Reid (eds.), *The Dictionary of Paul and his Letters* (Downers Grove: IVP, 1993)

Padgett, Alan, 'The Pauline Rationale for Submission: Biblical Feminism and the *hina* Clauses of Titus 2:1-10', *Evangelical Quarterly*, Vol. LIX, No. 1 (January, 1987)

Park, David M., 'The Structure of Authority in Marriage', *Evangelical Quarterly* Vol. LIX, No. 2 (April, 1987)

Pawson, J. David, *Leadership is Male* (Crowborough: Highland Books 1988)

Payne, Philip B., 'Libertarian women at Ephesus: A response to Douglas J. Moo's Article, '1 Timothy 2:11-15: Meaning and Significance',' *Trinity Journal* Vol. 2, No. 2 (1981)

Penner, Carol (ed.) *Women and Men: Gender in the Church*, (Scottdale / Waterloo: Herald Press, 1998)

Lloyd Pietersen, 'Women in the Pastorals' (Part 1), *Anabaptism Today* (Spring 1998), 'Women in the Pastorals' (Part 2), *Anabaptism Today* (Summer 1998)

Pinnock, Clark, *Flame of Love* (Downers Grove: IVP, 1997)

Poloma, Margaret, *The Assemblies of God at the Crossroads: Charisma and Institutional Dilemmas* (Knoxville: University of Tennessee, 1989)

Powell, Claire, 'A stalemate of genders? Some hermeneutical reflections', *Themelios*, Vol. 17, No. 3 (April / May, 1992)

Robertson, Archibald & Alfred Plummer, *1 Corinthians*, ICC series (Edinburgh: T & T Clark, 1971)

Robinson, J. Armitage, *St. Paul's Epistle to the Ephesians* (London / New York: MacMillan & Co., 1903)

Robson, Brenda, *The Turning Tide* (London: Marshall-Pickering, 1989)

Sanders, James, *From Sacred Story to Sacred Text: Canon as Paradigm* (Philadelphia: Fortress, 1987)

Spencer, F. Scott, *Acts*, Readings: A New Biblical Commentary (Sheffield: SAP, 1997)

Stevens, R. P., 'The mystery of male and female: Biblical and Trinitarian models', *Themelios* Vol. 17, No. 3 (April / May, 1992)

Swartley, Willard, *Slavery, Sabbath, War and Women* (Scottdale: Herald, 1983)

Swidler, Leonard, *Biblical Affirmations of Women* (Philadelphia: Westminster, 1979)

Thomas, Gordon, 'Telling a Hawk from a Handsaw? An Evangelical response to the New Literary Criticism' in *The Evangelical Quarterly*, Vol. LXXI / No. 1 (Jan. 1999), pp. 37-50

Thomas, John Christopher 'Women, Pentecostals and the Bible: An Experiment in Pentecostal Hermeneutics' *Journal of Pentecostal Theology*, Issue 5, (Sheffield: SAP, October 1994)

Turner, Max, *Power from on High*, Journal of Pentecostal Theology Supplement 9 (Sheffield: SAP, 1996)

Trible, Phyllis, *God and the Rhetoric of Sexuality*, Overtures to Biblical Theology, 2 (Philadelphia: Fortress, 1978)

Trombley, Charles, *Who said Women can't Teach* (South Plainfield: Logos, 1985)

Volf, Miroslav, *After Our Likeness: The Church as the Image of the Trinity* (Grand Rapids: Eerdmans, 1998)

Wilshire, Leland, '1 Timothy 2:12 Revisited: A Reply to Paul W. Barnett and Timothy J. Harris', *Evangelical Quarterly* Vol. LXV, No. 1 (January, 1993)

Wink, Walter, *Engaging the Powers* (Minneapolis: Fortress, 1992)

Witherington III, Ben, *Women and the Genesis of Christianity* (Cambridge: Cambridge University Press, 1990)

Wright, N. T., 'How Can the Bible be Authoritative', *Vox Evangelica* Vol. XXI (1991)

————— *The New Testament and the People of God* (Minneapolis: Fortress; London: SPCK, 1992)

————— 'The New Testament and the 'state',' *Themelios* Vol. 16, No. 1 (October / November, 1990)

Youngs, Dale, 'What's So Good About the Goddess?', *Christianity Today* (August 16, 1993)